The Turkey Hunter's Book

The Turkey Hunter's Book

BY JOHN M. McDANIEL

Illustrated with original photographs
from the author's private collection

Drawings by DONALD SHOFFSTALL

Authorized and for the benefit of
The National Wild Turkey Federation

The Amwell Press
CLINTON, NEW JERSEY
1980

Contents

] v [

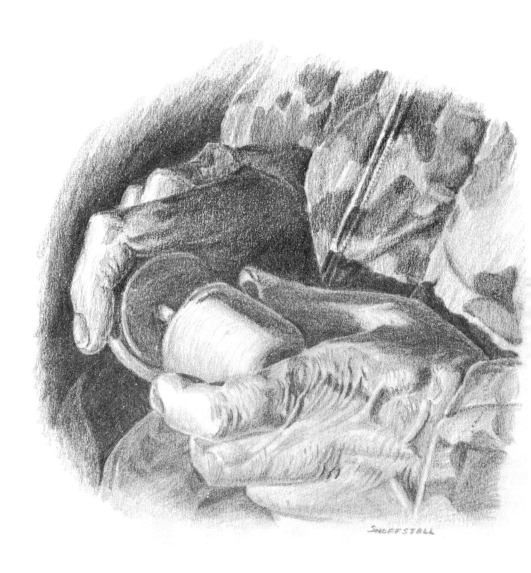

Acknowledgements

I'd like to thank the men and women with whom I've hunted turkeys. I've enjoyed their company and I've learned about turkeys from them.

I am indebted to the many property owners who have allowed me to hunt on their farms. Much of the information contained in this book was obtained by virtue of their generosity and trust.

There are three people who made it possible for me to undertake this book: my parents, Joseph and Eilleen McDaniel, and my wife, Nell Reeves McDaniel.

Neither of my parents are hunters. Both have supported my addiction from its first manifestations. Thanks exclusively to them, I have enjoyed the opportunity of using the finest equipment available. Thanks exclusively to them, I have a library of turkey literature and art of which I have seen no equal.

My wife, Nell, has continuously supported my turkey hunting. Rather than begrudging me the time I spend in the field, she encourages me to hunt. Rather than resenting my commitment, she celebrates my enjoyment.

Finally, a word of thanks to four people who helped with the maps, in the darkroom, and with the text. Three archaeology students from Washington and Lee University, Jim Adams, Parker Potter, and Kurt Russ spent their evenings with the turkey text after full days doing archaeological work. Jeannette Jarvis worked with many copies of the manuscript and never failed to decipher my handwriting, a task the three students claim is impossible.

Introduction

In writing this book, I have chosen not to follow the style of most how-to-hunt publications. I have considered some topics which are not a part of the traditional format and have omitted several which are. The book is structured around discrete topics—enhancing its value for reference.

The research upon which the book is based involved many hours of field observation and detailed analysis. For example, I tested ammunition with an Oheler 33 Chronograph purchased specifically to provide data for this book. All photographs were taken by me, my wife, or a hunting partner; moreover, all those of turkeys are of wild birds in their natural habitat.

At the risk of sounding abrasively critical, I am compelled to interject that I have read articles and books that have offered poor advice on turkey hunting. Poor advice can be encountered concerning any subject; however, in the field of wild turkey hunting the problem is compounded by the lack of experienced hunters who have questioned the errors. In this book, I have challenged ideas that tests and research have convinced me are erroneous.

I have no financial interest in or tie to any individual, or company, marketing products used by turkey hunters. The equipment I cite is mentioned by name because I believe it is excellent and that it will help you hunt more effectively.

I am confident that the time is right for this book. The 1980's promise to be great years for the wild turkey. Populations are on the rise but the decades ahead will present tremendous threats to turkey habitat. As we face these years, it is critical that we develop a dedication to the bird and his future that is at least equal to our commitment to the sport he provides.

The time has come for all American sportsmen to pledge themselves to upgrading the status of this unique game bird. Turkey hunters themselves must become aggressive proponents of their quarry. European hunters speak of their Auerhahn with reverence and awe, but an Auerhahn has no more of those qualities which make a bird game than a wild turkey. European, African, and Asian hunters should be encouraged to include the wild turkey on their list of most desirable trophies. Unlike the American representatives of the cat, deer, sheep, bear, grouse, quail, duck, and geese families, the wild turkey is totally distinctive from game native to other continents. The wild turkey deserves the title of king of the world's game birds.

The wild turkey is available. You probably live within a day's journey of excellent populations. Hunting the bird does not have to be expensive. All that you need to hunt successfully is a license, a modest amount of time, a modest collection of equipment, a large measure of determination, and a willingness to learn. It is my sincere hope that this book will help you.

The Turkey Hunter's Book

· 1 ·

In Praise of the Wild Turkey and Wild Turkey Hunters

Many eloquent men sing the praises of upland birds. They call the ruffed grouse king. They praise the bobwhite quail, the southern gentleman's bird. They describe the superb sport the woodcock provides for close working dogs and quick shooting men. They write of the ringnecked pheasant, claiming that this arrogant and adaptable immigrant will be the upland king of the immediate future.

Our candidate deserves the title of king of the uplands. He has great credentials but has received relatively little acclaim. Why? I believe the answer is simple—great turkey hunters are not eloquent men. The poet and the professor can fit their grouse into rich afternoons preceding productive evenings of writing. The turkey hunter's full day leaves no time or desire for eloquence in the evening. He moves to bed at an early hour, his body numb with the fatigue the demanding day has conferred.

Historically, the case for the wild turkey is strong. The American Indian, during the periods known to the archaeologist as the archaic and woodland, perceived the turkey as king. It was the turkey, not the smaller gallinaceous bird that was respected, valued, and even worshiped in the cultures of the pre-contact American Indians.

It was also the wild turkey that attracted the attention of the Spanish explorers. The smaller grouse, similar to the red-legged partridge of Spain, did not impress the Spanish; but the turkey was different. The bold, proud gobbler attracted the attention of the bold, proud conquistador. To have suggested to either the

American Indian or the early Spanish explorers that the wild turkey was not king of the American uplands would have been ludicrous.

Today the wild turkey suffers from the interest it stimulated during the earliest periods of European occupation of the New World. The domestication of the turkey was a tribute to its recognition as a valuable commodity and was economically a success; however, in the context of the status of the great bird it was a catastrophe. The sleek, beautiful, wary bird of the wilds evolved into the fat, ulgy, stupid butterball of captivity. The domestic turkey has become a symbol of stupidity. One of America's great minds, Benjamin Franklin, suggested the wild turkey as an appropriate symbol for our country. In 1776, the suggestion was viable; today the idea would be met with laughter. It is a historical tragedy that most contemporary Americans do not respect this great bird.

The wild turkey provides the greatest challenge that upland hunting offers. No other upland bird is as strong, fast, elusive, tough, wary, or clever. The difficulty inherent in killing a mature gobbler is sobering. If it were not for the existence of the spring season, when the bird is often blind with viril lust, mature gobblers would rarely be killed. In the fall, very few mature gobblers are harvested; moreover, ninety percent of those killed are taken by chance. Find a hunter who kills *mature* gobblers consistently in the fall and you will have an individual who should be a legend among his hunting colleagues. Young turkeys, even young gobblers, often do foolish things but, in the fall, a mature gobbler does not.

A king should be proud to the point of arrogance. The proudest and most arrogant of our upland birds is the mature wild turkey gobbler. There is no more defiant challenge, or bold summons, than the gobble of the male turkey. The strut of a gobbler in the spring is an exercise in elegance and dignity. The movements are measured and precise. The pride of the gobbler is a major factor increasing the difficulty of killing him during the mating season. A hunter in the spring can call with great skill only to be frustrated by the gobbler that demands the "hen" come to him. A gobbler expects hens to run to him. Even the most accomplished caller has difficulty in combating the gobbler's pride. It is only in frustration and with intense sexual desire that the gobbler ultimately moves to the hen. The successful spring hunter can enjoy the satisfaction of knowing that he has not only overcome the sagacity of his adversary but his pride and conceit as well.

A grouse hunter will state that the turkey cannot compare to their bird's beauty. The compact grouse is singularly beautiful, even in death; however, before you dismiss the turkey as ugly, take a measured look at a wild bird. Do not look at the many inaccurate prints which show the bird with small eyes and strange colors. Look at photographs of the mature bird with its enormous eyes, powerful legs, and broad spectrum of colors. Observe him alive. A turkey loses a great deal in death—the colors fade, the body stiffens, the head and neck are twisted in grotesque poses. Look at the living creature in clear photographs or in the few good prints.

The bird is capable of incredible physical feats. I have read that "the flight of a turkey is awkward." The statement is false. A turkey can flush with incomparable violence and thread its way through dense cover. The same turkey, in another setting, may leap off a ridge and sail across a valley with the speed of a driven pheasant. A grouse might fly three hundred yards on a long flight; a wild turkey will fly three thousand yards. No bird in the world combines such powerful flight with comparable running speed. The turkey runs with its head stretched out and its body low to the ground. The long legs seem to reach beyond the bird. No imagination is so vivid as to provide an accurate picture of the speed attained by a healthy turkey sprinting across open terrain.

Despite his size, the turkey's coordination and grace are astounding. If you doubt the coordination possessed by this creature, watch one walk cautiously through the leaf cover of a late fall woods. In such a situation, every step the turkey takes is deliberate; often the large foot is held up in the air for long seconds before it is placed down.

If you have been impressed by the pheasant's ability to hide, I hope you have an opportunity to watch a twenty-pound gobbler stretch out flat in minimal cover and disappear from view. I once saw a flock of twelve birds hide in a harvested field in which the only growth was stubble six inches high. The turkey is also capable of almost noiseless flight. Although it is true that a gobbler can crash through brush with a violence that makes the flush of a grouse seem tame, the same bird can pitch off his roost and glide to the ground without a sound.

Many tales have been told about the acuity of the turkey's vision. The experienced hunter learns that a turkey will see into all but the most impenetrable blind. Hunters also learn that an attempt to raise a gun slowly while a bird is visible will result in a shot at the tail of a rapidly departing turkey. Even the experienced hunter will be baffled by situations in which he sits motionless, in a good blind, and an approaching turkey will flush for no apparent reason. In such cases, it is no doubt the incredible vision of the bird that has literally penetrated the blind.

The hearing of a turkey is as keen as his vision. The caller's softest yelp will often stimulate a gobble from a distant ridge. Frequently it will be hard for the hunter to believe that the distant, barely perceptible gobble is in response to his call.

The immensity of the challenge provided by turkey hunting is compounded by the difficulty inherent in killing this great creature. The strength and tenacity of a mature turkey are awesome. Many men respect the pheasant for its ability to survive grave wounds. The pheasant is a very tough bird, but a turkey is much more difficult to kill. If you think a wounded pheasant is elusive, wait until you have seen a winged turkey. A mature gobbler will outrun a pheasant the way a cheetah would outrun a bobcat.

Many intelligent, honest men will argue that no bird is as good on the table as a ruffed grouse. Again I ask you to compare a wild turkey to the grouse. I will not make a case for one being superior to the other because both are superb. From a gustatory standpoint, no other game bird compares to either a young grouse or a young turkey.

The final case for the wild turkey, and perhaps the best, involves the areas in which he is sought. This great bird inhabits those precious still-wild regions of this country. He lives on rocky, cold hardwood ridges, in damp, warm southern swamps, and on bare, arid western plateaus. He does not tolerate the destruction of his environment. He is not a bird of game farms or "semi-wild" preserves. I have read about pen-raised turkeys that have been released to be shot in fields; such an exercise is obscene and is no closer to turkey hunting than shooting sheep in a pen is to sheep hunting.

In that still wild upland realm that the turkey oversees, he is the king. The remainder of this work is dedicated to helping you prepare to seek him. A trip to a remote area of the world is not necessary; in fact, it is impossible to find him outside the Americas. You will not have to travel far but he may ask much more of you than game that demands you travel thousands of miles and spend thousands of dollars.

Turkey Hunters

The turkey selects turkey hunters. The process has selected men who enjoy a blend of physical toughness, intelligence, and determination. The great turkey hunters I know laugh when I suggest that they write about the bird they chase. One is a native West Virginian who speaks with a soft mountain accent. He lives to hunt wild turkeys. His occupation, that of a forester, allows him to be close to these birds he loves. During last year's spring season James had twenty possible calendar days for hunting. He hunted on eighteen. On each of those mornings, he was up at two-thirty to face the demanding hills of eastern West Virginia. He is an accomplished caller and splendid shot. Last spring, he failed to kill a gobbler. He was neither surprised nor distraught.

In many small mountain communities, the respect the turkey hunter earns cuts across sub-cultural boundaries based on sex. I have heard the proud wife or mother say, with unusual boldness, "James hunts nothing but turkeys; he doesn't fool with anything else." Mountain women boast of men who kill turkeys regularly.

Wherever he is and in whatever cultural situation he lives, the turkey hunter is in a class by himself. He enjoys this status in both the warm den of the prestigious hunting club and in the drab barbershop in the bleak Appalachian town. One is not a turkey hunter by virtue of killing a turkey or even a few turkeys; on the contrary, turkeys fall to deer hunters and squirrel hunters with a regularity that disturbs turkey hunters. One acquires the status of turkey hunter by demonstrating consistent success. To achieve this measure of success, a degree of specialization must be developed. It is nice to talk of how in May one can hunt turkeys in the morning and fish for trout in the afternoon; however, if you expect to kill your gobbler regularly in the spring you will fish very little. You must invest full days for consistent success with spring gobblers. The season may end at 11 a.m., but you have to scout in the afternoons and practice your calling in the evenings. In addition, the 2:30 a.m. alarm will dampen the enthusiasm with which one awaits the 3:30 p.m. hatch of mayflies. The turkey asks a lot. The successful turkey hunter pays his dues.

Turkeys demand the development and maintenance of stamina in the hunter. I have hunted turkeys with accomplished college athletes and they have suffered under the strain. If you wonder what the rigors of a sheep hunt are like, try a turkey in the rugged ridges of our Appalachian states. If you kill grouse with your legs, you kill turkeys with your heart.

The grouse hunter will, with accuracy, state that his bird also demands dedication and hard work. The distinguishing element is the level of patience required. The grouse hunter often hunts for a long time between flushes but he rarely goes days without seeing a bird. The best turkey hunter anticipates days without encountering game. He develops the quiet dedication of the salmon fisherman. Both men are addicted to the pursuit of the difficult. The nature of the game, be it salmon or turkey, provides one with the strength to face the incredibly long periods between contact with the quarry. The turkey hunter can appreciate the sense of satisfaction and fulfillment that the salmon specialist feels after having fished a stream well without moving a fish. Does even the most avid grouse hunter reflect with satisfaction on a day when no bird is flushed? I submit that this difference is a measure of the status of salmon to other fish and the wild turkey to other birds, even grouse.

One of the most important skills, the art of calling the wild turkey, was first practiced by the American Indian hundreds and even thousands of years ago. Today, nothing indicates a turkey can be fooled more easily; on the contrary, there are those who would suggest the challenge has increased with greater hunting pressure. Despite what the salesmen of turkey calls may state, it is not easy.

The turkey will not be consistently harvested by poor shooters. The vulnerable parts of the bird are small. If you use a shotgun, the turkey will teach you the modest range at which such a weapon is lethal. If you read about eighty-yard turkey guns, the piece was written by someone who doesn't know how difficult a turkey is to kill. You can quote pattern densities all day but any turkey that is over sixty yards from the shooter has a good chance of surviving a shot regardless of gauge, choke, load, or shot size. With a rifle, you have to be able to shoot accurately to kill turkeys. The modest skill that has been developed by many efficient deer hunters is just not adequate.

If turkey hunters, as a group, have a weakness it is a proclivity to avocational arrogance. The respect the turkey hunter allocates to hunters of other games is measured. Deer hunting is perceived as an activity best suited to adolescents, the infirm, the fat, and the old. In response to the question, "Why don't you hunt deer?" a wiry turkey hunter raised his light blue eyes to the interrogator and said:

> Any fool can kill a deer every year. He just finds himself a trail, sits down and, sooner or later, some impatient fellow from the city will chase one up the trail. The deer won't see the boy and the deer's mind ain't quick enough to convince him what to do about that boy's smell. So, the deer gawks at the smell and stamps his feet at it. Now if that good old boy don't get too nervous he will fill the scope up with the body of the deer and kill him.

> A turkey hunter, don't you see, he goes out and *hunts* a turkey. He don't depend on tree stands, or drives, or city fellows to push a half-blind animal to him. A turkey hunter has to be *smart enough* to know where the flock will be, *tough enough* to get close to scatter the birds, *clever enough* to put his blind in the right place, and *talented enough* to call a bird up. Now,

after he has done all that he better know how to sit *still* and be patient. Finally, when that bird is there, he better shoot *straight* and *quick* because a turkey's head and neck are small and even a young one won't stand there gawking at you and stamping his feet.

PORTRAIT OF A TURKEY HUNTER

James is a turkey hunter. In his part of West Virginia, no sentence says more about him. James is not a member of the N.R.A., he belongs to no hunt club, he subscribes to no outdoor journals, he does not hunt turkeys for human companionship. The loud, crowded, aggressively masculine hunt camp is as uncomfortable to him as an urban bar.

James lives to hunt turkeys. His is the legacy of the hunter that historians say helped shape the nation's character and that anthropologists argue helped establish the path of human evolution.

James has been captured, perhaps seduced, by both the challenge that the wild turkeys present and the comfort he derives from being embraced by those wild areas the turkey inhabits. James knows he is good at hunting turkeys and he is proud of it. He takes great satisfaction from the fact he is the best turkey hunter in Randolph County. He is neither a hermit nor a recluse. His tax statement says that he is a forester. In fact, he is a turkey hunter who works as a forester because his culture does not subsidize hunting. He works hard as a forester. Unfortunately, the diligent performance of his job provides less satisfaction and less public acclaim than that which accrues from his exploits as a superb turkey hunter.

James lives for November and April. During November, his days average eighteen hours in length. He gets no overtime—he asks for none. He eats, sleeps, and hunts. On many occasions he sleeps and eats only enough to be able to hunt. In the spring, turkeys begin to gobble at 4:30 a.m. To be in position at the top of a 3,000-foot ridge, you have to wake at 2:30. I know; I've hunted with James. The season is thirty days in length. He rarely misses more than a day. The last day of the spring season he will look like the GI after Anzio or one of Napoleon's boys on the road back from Moscow. He will have hunted to the edge of exhaustion. He occasionally falls over that edge.

He enjoys the fact that turkeys are tough. In James' words, he appreciates the fact "they make you bleed a little." Have you ever tried to climb up a mile-long, 60-degree slope in 70 degree April heat, bearing thirty pounds of clothes and equipment? Your legs cramp, your body aches, you wonder what the strain will do to a forty-year-old heart. You slip, and the equipment pounds you onto the sharp limestone and you grunt with very real pain. You get a sick feeling as you look up at the dark and distant ridge. Finally, you reach the ridge, find the tree, and sink into the cool ground. You let your body collapse and you feel your heart still struggle with the strain imposed by the climb. You look over the now lighter valley. You are proud of the perspective. You smile at James. He smiles back. This is the essential companionship of human hunting. Two men attempting something difficult together. Two friends who respect each other and celebrate each others success, and are sensitive to each others failures. This is not the raucous companionship of the deer camp where petty jealousy and envy turn cooperation into meaningless competition.

The gobble makes the climb inconsequential. Myriad years of human evolution have provided James with the mind and body to respond to the gobble. Instantly, he is alert and capable. He registers the distance to the bird and plans the attack with skill and speed. Gentle, soft-spoken, James is transformed into the most effective predator in the animal world. He runs toward the bird with agility and determination. His mind weighs all the necessary information. How far is the bird? How old is he? Where would it be best to call from? Is he still on the roost? His brain is James' greatest physical asset. The brain evolved in response to the need to perform such tasks.

James knows what it takes to kill turkeys regularly. He derives a sense of self-worth from his hunting success. They can call him lucky but he knows better. He has confidence in himself and knows that luck does not put his turkeys on the ground. His success and the reputation which accompanies it are based exclusively on his competence. Dress, articulateness, wealth, formal education, social position, or being an effective braggart have no relevance to his success. His accomplishments are earned and they are meaningful to his reputation. This is not killing a deer blinded by fear of an army of hunters. James knows the men of hunting camps are not efficient hunters. He encounters them occasionally. They are either sitting in trees in silent ambush, incapable of more skillful hunting, or they barge through the woods, loud, laden with sidearms and huge knives; an obscene parody of the efficient and proud human hunter.

Turkey hunting selects against the incompetent. Oh, the incompetent will enjoy occasional success but they are not capable of consistent success under fair conditions. In most cultures, only the consistently successful hunters are allocated the respect of their peers. James avoids the incompetent in the woods. They are dangerous.

I sat with James once and listened to a man call at James with his recently purchased box call. The man was very excited because he was sure James' call had been a turkey. I thought it was funny. James wasn't amused. "That boy may fire a shot up here after a while. Then he will go back to his camp and say he called one up close. They've shot at me a time or two. I wish these hills were even steeper so that we could get away from all of them all the time."

A day with James will provide a better testimony to the skill of human hunters than watching a movie of bushmen killing a giraffe in the Kalahari Desert. Have you ever heard a really good turkey hunter run a call? I don't like to watch James when he calls. He goes into himself. The blue eyes focus on something distant. The tone is unbelievable. He sounds exactly like a turkey. No better testimony can be made to the skill of human hunters than to hear a good one with a call.

James does not take the killing of turkeys as being secondary to some mystic experience of relating to the woods. James loves to *kill* turkeys. He talks about the times he has called birds up and not killed them.

"I don't know why, but it's not the same. You know the time

you took those photographs of the birds. It just wasn't the same. I like to be looking down the rib of the old Ithaca. I call better. You know I love my turkeys and I've passed up killing hens and young birds. But most of all I enjoy killing them. It hasn't diminished at all. I still like to carry them out of the woods."

James is a wonderful woodsman and when in the woods he is not oblivious to other creatures. I have watched him as he enjoyed the frolicking of young squirrels. He does not kill to answer some twisted need.

One summer evening when riding up to the mountain to search for young turkeys, we encountered a huge timber rattlesnake on the side of the road. James backed up to look at the snake and the rattler came for the big four-wheel drive vehicle. James said, with obvious admiration and respect, "This truck is a thousand times bigger than he is but that boy is standing his ground." It would have been easy to kill the snake and it would have made the local newspapers. James never considered killing it.

James' turkey gun is a 10-gauge Ithaca double he bought at a hardware store in Elkins, in 1936. He had seen one a man from New York had brought to hunt turkeys with and the hardware store owner ordered a similar gun. He has killed 118 turkeys with the gun. "Don't figure how many birds that works out to a year because it might be a bird or two over the limit," he once said with a smile. The gun fits the man. It is a credit to American ingenuity and craftsmanship.

The gun is not as pretty as a Purdey but this is an American gun. It was made for honest, decent men who were not born of noble lineage. When its price tag was $100 the Purdey sold for $1000. It is a testimony to the democratic nature of American hunting. The 10½-pound gun is a collector's item—like its owner, it is authentic. It is a reminder of a period when fine American shotguns were made by hand, by men who cared.

It's interesting that the few great turkey hunters I know are armed with old Model 12 Winchesters, Browning automatics made in Belgium, L. C. Smiths, big Parkers, and pre-1964 Model 70 Winchesters in 22 Hornet. These guns were made for people like James. The semi-wild preserves select for impressed checkering, plastic butt plates, stamped metal and men who have been weaned on preserves and plastic guns.

James exists—right now he is probably working with his calls. The big Ithaca, carefully cleaned, hangs in his modest home.

In other sections of this county, proud guns hang waiting to be used by capable men and women. Their hunting knowledge and competence will match that of any rich German in the Black Forest. These hunters provide proof of the fact that contemporary hunting still requires the development of skills and capabilities. Hunting for these Americans provides enjoyment, satisfaction, and fulfillment.

· 2 ·

Wild Turkey Biology and Behavior Relevant to Hunting

This section will not summarize the life cycle of the wild turkey. Subjects such as fertilization of eggs, the incubation process, the behavior of poults when they hatch, details of summer flock structure, disease threats, and the nature of sub-specific population variations will not be discussed. These subjects are presented in many of the works listed in the bibliography. Here we shall be concerned only with those aspects of wild turkey behavior of specific relevance to hunting.

GREGARIOUSNESS

Turkeys begin their lives in a group. Survival of the immature turkey is dependent upon the bird staying with the group. The hen not only provides the poult with protection against numerous predators but also acts as a shield from inclement weather. The hen constantly checks on the location of the members of her brood. The number in the brood will vary but in many instances the hen will begin a summer with ten to fourteen energetic poults.

During the earliest stage, the birds learn that the flock means security and isolation is to be avoided. The first calls of the young bird are essentially designed to maintain contact with the hen and other members of the brood. The curiosity of the young turkeys will stimulate the birds to investigate the flora and fauna they encounter. The young bird that suddenly realizes it has become isolated from the flock will begin to whistle frantically. The hen will respond with her call and the young bird will sprint to her.

As the poult matures, the concept of group security is enforced. During the fall, the now full-sized poults, of both sexes, are still members of their mother's brood group. Their separation from the group, despite the fact that the distances involved may be much greater, initiates the same drive to return to the company of the hen and the other poults.

It is this highly developed drive to reestablish contact with the group which makes the young bird highly susceptible to calling after the scattering of a flock in the fall and winter.

The hunter should be aware that several hens and their respective broods will often travel together in an aggregate brood flock of large size. There are invariably the flocks of eighty birds reported by men who are in the field in the months of August, September and October. It is very hard to count the number of birds as these large flocks move. In most instances, these flocks will be observed in open fields. One of the most frustrating tasks is trying to count aggressive young turkeys as they dart back and forth after grasshoppers. Many of the claims of flock size are exaggerations. The largest flock I have seen held about 40 birds. I will hasten to add that in thirty minutes of observation I made four counts of the flock and came up with numbers of 46, 43, 44, and 45. In the flock, four birds were obviously mature hens; so I assume this was a group of four hens with their large broods.

It is during these first summer months the turkeys are alive that this drive for the company of other turkeys becomes an important aspect of their behavior. Despite the many stories of hermit gobblers, the desire for the company of other turkeys remains an important behavioral attribute of both sexes—a drive which for most gobblers is only disrupted by the mating season.

Most mature gobblers spend the fall and winter season in the company of other mature gobblers. Granted these male fraternities are small; often they will consist of only three or four birds, but they constitute important groups. The adult gobblers strive to maintain the groups, and the scattering of one of their flock sets the stage for the hunter to call the old birds.

THE DIET

Turkeys enjoy the luxury of not being dependent on a single food source. It is true that in many areas the acorn is the turkey's favorite food; however, in a poor mast year the turkey will adjust to many other foods. The catholic diet should be appreciated by the hunter. It is important to know what foods are used and when.

Biological texts and the fine studies that are published by wildlife management units can be invaluable aids; however, do not underestimate your own ability to add knowledge about the specific area in which you hunt. For example, I discovered that paw-paw was a very popular fall food in a county where I hunt. This is one food that has received little mention in the literature. Another example is the young gobbler's reliance on animal food in the spring season. Most of the young gobblers I have examined in the spring have newts and salamanders in their craws.

Each bird you have access to can teach you something about the diet. Don't be embarrassed to ask to see the craw of a friend's bird—offer to clean it for him. You will learn a great deal by carefully studying each bird that you have access to.

A knowledge of the nature of the bird's diet gives you a direct clue to where he will be. With the exception of the abnormal behavior during the spring, the bird will be close to the preferred and available sources of food. Obviously the food must be available to be used. The hunter who sits in ambush in a grape thicket with no grapes on the vines is not hunting intelligently. He will not kill a turkey in that cover because the turkey is too smart to look for food he knows isn't there.

The intelligent hunter will also be aware that the turkey may search out specific food sources as dictated by weather. Heavy snow may see birds working the exposed grape vines rather than attempting to scratch for mast under snow drifts.

Learn the types of food turkeys use in your area and try to determine which the bird will be dependent upon the next time you hunt.

WEATHER

The adult wild turkey will survive all but the longest or most violent storms. Deep snow, bitter cold, high winds and intense heat rarely result in adult mortality. Those of us who are concerned about the welfare of the birds will wonder if a particularly harsh storm hasn't eliminated turkeys. Usually, the answer is that the turkeys will have survived the storm.

During the first two months of its life, the young turkey is vulnerable to fluctuations in weather. Summer rains, thunder showers, and unseasonably cool weather often cause high mortality in broods. The small bird does not enjoy the heat maintenance system of the adult. If a poult becomes wet, it is difficult for it to maintain body temperature. If the wet bird is subjected to cool temperatures and winds, the effect is more serious. The hen tries to protect the poults with her wings and by keeping them close to her own warm body; however, the hen can only be so effective. There is no question that in most good turkey ranges the most important single factor influencing population size from one year to the next is the weather during the critical months just after the hatching of the poults. Unfortunately, it is not the general weather pattern during this period that is the key but rather the timing and severity of a few summer storms.

The intelligent hunter must be cognizant of the effects weather has on the birds he hunts. Despite reports to the contrary, I rarely find turkeys that stay on the roost for days during inclement weather. I have encountered turkeys feeding in the middle of intense storms. The morning after a snow storm is one on which birds will usually be feeding. I have found too many flocks the morning after a storm to accept the idea that "they stay on the roost for a full day after a snow."

I do not like to hunt in high winds, but, my success seems to be less affected by wind than is the case with other species of game. I'd rather hunt turkeys in still weather but in high wind I am confident they do not become as cautious as game that depends on its sense of smell.

Turkeys do not always stop gobbling when it rains. I have no answer to what it is that makes for a good gobbling morning, I'm not sure the gobbler himself knows. However, I have learned that you can enjoy success in the rain.

I do believe that turkeys will respond better to a call, or at least they will respond a bit quicker, on mornings when a mist or fog clings to the ground. The birds seem more willing to come closer to the call than they do in sharp, clear days. From my experience, the last comment applies to the spring as well as to the fall season.

I like dry woods and still days. I can hear turkeys better under such conditions; besides, I'm never going to move up on any without being heard under any weather conditions. Oh, I've walked into my share of fall flocks but on all these occasions I am confident the turkeys heard the movement I made but they simply hadn't determined it was a threat.

WARINESS, VISUAL AND AUDITORY ACUITY AND INTELLIGENCE

One reads of the acute senses, great instincts, and innate wariness possessed by wild turkeys. Turkeys do have marvelous senses of vision and hearing. To state that their vision or hearing is eight, ten, or X times better than that of humans is inane. There are no tests that would allow such an appraisal. Suffice it to say that the hearing and vision of turkeys are superb. As important as the sharpness of their senses is the *speed* with which they determine that something is a threat.

It is unquestionable that the turkey's fear of human predation is learned. Historical accounts from the eighteenth and nineteenth centuries indicate that the bird's response to humans was far different than it is today; moreover, there are contemporary populations that show less fear of humans. While the wild turkey I encountered was a different bird taxonomically, my experience during two years in the Peruvian jungles indicated that the turkey unfamiliar with humans can be as gullible as any wilderness grouse. I am confident that ten years of intensive hunting in Peru would alter the behavior of the turkey. The alterations in behavior would produce a much more wary bird.

The bird is capable of learning. If you don't believe this, spend a week working spring gobblers just before the season. If you call a couple of birds to you and then let them know they have been fooled by standing up and yelling at them, see how easy those birds are to call back. I've photographed birds before our spring season and it has always been hard for me to get the same birds to come to my calling during the season.

Turkeys have been called stupid for returning to the same feeding area after receiving heavy hunting pressure in the fall. In fairness to the bird, when food is limited to a few covers the bird has little choice but to use those areas.

Turkeys also enjoy a measure of wariness that is not characteristic of many popular forms of North American game. The turkey comes by this wariness naturally. Unlike deer, the turkey still has many natural predators. Most good turkey ranges have healthy populations of bobcats, foxes, owls, and hawks. All these will prey on turkeys. If you question the hawks as not deserving membership on the list, I can state that I have seen two wild turkeys attacked by a hawk. I'm not speaking of poults either; both birds I saw attacked were full grown. What legitimate natural predator exists for deer in most of their ranges? In most situations, feral dogs are the only non-human threat to deer.

The turkey's vulnerability has selected for birds that are cautious and quick to flee what they define as dangerous. Turkeys do not often stand and stare at the unfamiliar. When something does not fit, they flee.

I submit that you can hunt the entire world and you will not find a creature that is more wary than a mature gobbler during the fall and winter season. He never relaxes. The speed with which the old gobbler reacts to what he defines as dangerous is amazing. The instant an approaching gobbler sees something is out of place he will throw himself backwards and take flight in one violent motion.

While blessed with strength and endurance, the turkey has no biological weapons of defense. Deer, in contrast, can make life difficult for predators with their hooves. The turkey also suffers from being conspicuous. If aware of danger he can hide, but when feeding he is particularly obvious.

MATING BEHAVIOR

During the spring the mating instincts of both hens and gobblers stimulates a restructuring of behavior. The gregariousness that characterized the bird's behavior is dramatically altered as the birds establish discreet areas in which they spend a significant period of time alone.

The adult gobbler's separation from the other gobblers he has traveled with during the fall and winter begins when he establishes his courting area. From this location, he attempts to attract hens for the purpose of breeding. The signal he uses to announce his presence to the hens, and to any competing males, is the gobble. The successful male will usually attract and hold several hens.

During the spring, the male is obsessed with mating. Biologically, he acquires a sponge of fat in his breast area which provides a caloric reserve during the time he is too busy to eat. The gobbler's spring consists of gobbling, displaying, mating, and preparing to do all three.

It is rare that gobblers will engage in combat with other males. Two or more gobblers will be seen together with hens and the males will appear to be oblivious to one another. Often the birds will strut and display in what seems to be a rehearsed performance. Most of the time spent by gobblers in the company of hens is spent in display. The birds literally strut until they wear the tips of their primary feathers down to rough and broken ends. By observing the mating ritual for an extended period of time you can appreciate how much more time is dedicated to the strut and display than to actual mating.

Most gobbling occurs before the hens go to the gobbler early in the morning. The gobbler will occasionally gobble while with hens but more frequently he will not. If the hens, after being serviced, move back to their nests, the gobbler may attempt to attract other birds by beginning to gobble actively again. Also, the silent gobbler, in the middle of his elegant display, may be encouraged to gobble if he hears the call of a distant hen.

The life of the young—one-year-old—gobbler is characterized

by seclusion in the spring. The young gobbler has not achieved the sexual maturity of the adult bird. He does not enjoy the breast fat deposit and consequently spends a considerable amount of time feeding. The young gobbler becomes very elusive in the spring and will often come silently to the hunter. Early in the spring he will be found in the company of hens but as the season progresses and the hens spend more time on their nests the young gobbler will live a solitary existence. He will occasionally come to the call of a hen and he will make an attempt at gobbling. Most of the time he acts as if he is not sure what his role is.

THE HEN IN THE SPRING

During the spring, the first-year hen comes of age. Unlike her sibling males, she engages in the mating activities and her behavior becomes similar to that of the adult hens. She seeks out the gobbler and accompanies him for the mating ritual; subsequently, she will build a nest and lay eggs. As the cluster of eggs grows she will stay with them around the clock, except for a break for food and water in the afternoon.

One of the keys to successful spring hunting is to learn when most hens begin to stay with their clutches of eggs. This will occur approximately the same time each year. This is the time when the gobblers will suddenly find fewer hens responding to their charms. Their response is to search out the reluctant hen. Hunting is much easier during this phase of the season. There will be a *hot week* that corresponds to the time that this alteration in hen behavior takes place. It is critical that the spring hunter learns when this takes place in his areas.

COMMUNICATION

The gregarious and intelligent nature of the wild turkey is the key to the evolution of its complex system of communication. Unlike many other birds, the turkey has developed numerous signals. The complex, and often discussed, pattern of vocal communication is only one system that is used.

NON-VOCAL COMMUNICATION

Perceptive hunters have learned that mechanically produced sounds are used by turkeys for communication. One of the most common sounds is made by scratching the ground in a manner which imitates the turkey's food-searching behavior. Birds that have been subjected to heavy hunting pressure, particularly if that pressure involves frequent calling, will communicate by scratching in the leaves. This form of communication is often displayed in the fall of the year by mature gobblers that have been scattered. The sounds made by turkeys scratching can be imitated by the hunter. The key to imitating the sounds is to recognize that the birds maintain a distinct rhythm. Frequently, three distinct raking strokes will be made with a slightly longer delay between the second and third strokes.

The hunter can make a very effective imitation of the raking action. The first time it is attempted one's hunting companions may display either contempt or amusement; however, the judicious use of the technique can help fool birds that have developed an exaggerated measure of caution. This mechanical form of communication can also be used in conjunction with vocal calls. It is particularly effective when it follows a single vocal call which attracts a bird's attention.

Another mechanical form of communication is made by the birds as they walk through the noisy ground cover characteristic of many habitats. Anyone who has called birds knows that the sounds of their walking can be surprisingly loud. Occasionally, the hunter will believe the bird is much closer than it is in fact because of the volume and clarity of the sounds made by the bird walking. The sound is similar to that made by a man walking. The similarities are a function of the common two-legged gait; however, it is rare that an experienced hunter will not be able to decipher between the sounds of a man and a turkey. When the bird is moving at a regular gait, the pace is quicker. Also, the individual steps will be more regular and there will be an absence of the occasionally loud sounds made by a man. In the spring of the year, the old gobbler can be deceived by the clever hunter who develops a pace and walking style that imitates the sounds made by a turkey. The gobbler expects the hen to move to his seductive gobbles; hence, if the hunter is in a position which places a topographical feature between himself and the bird, he can use the imitative walking pace to convince the gobbler the hen is moving to him. The distance at which the gobbler can pick up the sounds is incredible.

A good friend, and extremely competent hunter, fooled one bird that had frustrated him for three successive mornings by using footsteps alone. When the bird gobbled my friend positioned himself just over a small rise from the bird and without making a single call moved toward the gobbling bird. My friend walked ten to fifteen yards at a time, trying to imitate the quick pace and light but distinct steps of a hen turkey. The gobbler responded to the sound of the approaching hunter by gobbling much more excitedly. When my friend was close to the top of the small ridge, he stopped and hid himself in a convenient natural blind. After several more minutes of frantic gobbling, the aggravated tom pitched to the top of the ridge and walked within range.

In some situations, such as the one just related, the mechanical call can be used exclusively to fool turkeys; however, in most cases it is best used as a supplement to vocal calls. No matter how it is used, or even if it is not used, the accomplished hunter should be aware that turkeys communicate with non-vocal sounds.

VISUAL COMMUNICATION

The ritual of the adult gobbler in the spring is a clear testimony to the importance of vision in the communication of the wild turkey. While the gobble and the drumming sounds of the strut are important components of the sexual display of the male, the changes in the bird that are only perceptible by vision are critical. Color, shape, and movement are essential to the display.

The posture of turkeys can also indicate a state of relaxation, anxiety, aggressiveness, fear, or terror. The high neck, high head position indicates anxiety just as readily as a sharp cluck.

Birds maintain visual contact while feeding on the ground and often will communicate to another bird only after seeing it. The importance of vision in communication is made very clear to the hunter who watches the speed with which the spring gobbler will fly to the hen that steps out into an open glade or flys close to the base of his roosting tree. Young birds in the fall often use their wonderful vision to regroup after being scattered by a hunter or other predator. I have often watched, with disappointment, as a whole flock flushed through the canopy of the woods and re-grouped in the air before landing hundreds of yards away.

The only hunting technique that has been developed that directly addresses the visual communication of the birds is the use of decoys—of course, the importance of camouflage and conceal-ment is an effective testimony to the importance of the visual acu-ity of the birds. The hen decoy can be used to lure the reluctant gobbler to the hunter in the spring season. I do not use decoys nor do I intend to in the future. The decision not to use them does not suggest that I do not acknowledge the significance of visual com-munication, but rather that I believe the decoy would only be a valuable advantage in one out of fifty situations encountered. The problems involved in transporting it would be considerable, and the threat of some idiot shooting at the decoy is a very real one.

A knowledge of the dependence placed on visual communica-tion by the wild turkey can help the hunter offset the obvious se-curity advantages that this sytem affords the birds.

VOCAL COMMUNICATION

The wild turkey uses many vocal signals for communication. The tone, rhythm, volume, pitch and quality of the sounds are dependent on the age, sex, nature of the message being communi-cated, and the individual quality of a particular bird's call.

There are several basic calls that every hunter should be able to identify.

THE WHISTLE OF THE YOUNG BIRD

The whistle is an important call of young birds of both sexes. As with all calls, there are individual variations on the basic pattern; however, the most frequently heard form is a rising and shrill three-note whistle that can be imitated by saying *tee-tee-teeee* or *key-key-keeeee*. The volume increases on the third note and all the notes should be made in the same breath. If one inhales between the notes, the delay will be too great.

This call is made by the tiny poults as soon as they are hatched. The rhythm used by the young birds is similar to that which they will use when, six months later, they will be legal game for fall hunters. The tone, pitch, and volume will change. There are several variations on the basic whistle that every hunter should know. At times these variations will be based on a bird's individual idiosyncracies, while others will be based on the nature of the circumstance stimulating the call. For example, a young bird that is eager for the company of the flock from which it has been scattered will often put a long sequence of the whistles together in a call that effectively communicates the anxiety of the lost bird. As the birds enter their first fall the whistles will often be preceded or followed by rough yelps. In general, the young gobbler will develop a call that is characterized by a series of clear whistles which runs right into a sequence of deep yelps. The young hen, on reaching the age five or six months (when most turkey seasons begin) may depend exclusively upon a three or four note series of high-pitched yelps. There are exceptions to this disparity by sex, but the experienced hunter can often use it to identify the sex of the young turkey he hears. The whistle is primarily a fall call, but it will occasionally be heard in the spring. In these cases, it is usually the yearling gobbler that will use it in conjunction with other calls, one of which is often his discordant gobble.

THE CLUCK

To gain a fair perception of what a cluck sounds like, place the tip of your tongue against the roof of your mouth and say the word "tuck" very quickly. This sound is again used by birds of both sexes and in a variety of contexts. It is often used for close communication by birds that may have used yelps to get close to each other. The posture of the bird and the tone of the cluck connotes the question, "Is that you?" when there is an implicit confidence in the response.

The cluck will often be used by birds that are reluctant to rely on yelps. Mature gobblers in the fall will often communicate with one another with clucks rather than yelps. Also, birds of all ages will refrain from yelping and depend on clucks after being subjected to heavy hunting pressure in the fall. It is quite common to have young birds run quickly to a few soft clucks late in the fall season.

The cluck is also used for communication in the spring. It is frequently made by birds as they first awake on the roost. There are gobblers who will come to soft clucks after spurning the more popular hen yelps.

It is true that the cluck, used either in the fall or the spring, can repel birds if the hunter interjects a sense of alarm in his call. There are many experienced and successful hunters who feel the distinction between the interrogative cluck and the alarm cluck, often called a putt, is so small that the cluck should not be used. I have called too many birds with this call to accept this argument as valid. The call must be used with care but it can be very effective.

THE PUTT

The alarm putt, referred to in the last paragraph, is the turkey's way of concisely saying, "Danger, get out of here." The reader can gain a fair appraisal of this sound by preparing to make the cluck as described above; but before making the sound, tighten your stomach muscles and then eject the sound with force. Also the typical alarm call will be a rapid series of this high sharp note. Make these sounds as quickly as you can and then accept the fact a turkey's will be sharper and quicker.

THE GOBBLE

This special call is only made by the male. It is made in the fall as well as the spring and by immature, first-year gobblers as well as mature birds. In the fall, it is made less frequently than in the spring; however, I have hunted some young gobblers that used the call regularly in the fall. These birds combined the call with the more typical whistles; and to suggest they used it infrequently would be wrong.

The call is used to attract hens in the spring. Birds vary in the degree to which they use this call. I have listened to a gobbler make over 180 gobbles in a 45-minute period. In this case, the bird gobbled almost without pause. Other gobblers are characteristically economical in their use of the gobble. The tone and pitch of the gobbling sound varies in a somewhat regular manner with respect to the age of the bird, but there are also individual variations not dependent on age. In general, the older bird will have a clearer and more distinct gobble. Some immature birds make strange sounds as they struggle to master this call.

The call of the wild bird only sounds like the gobble-gobble-gobble noise we are familiar with as children if you run the notes together very quickly and add a staccato rhythm to the sequence.

THE YELP

The yelp is the basic call of the turkey for communicating at distances beyond 100 yards. Hence to the hunter, who by necessity must be at some distance, it becomes a most important call.

The sound can best be approximated by the novice by slurring the word "yonk" as a two-syllable word. If the word is said distinctly, it would sound nothing like the yelp. If the word is slurred and if a somewhat higher note is interjected in the first syllable, a fair imitation will be achieved. String several of these in a row and a basic sequence will be achieved.

The most interesting aspect of the yelp is its many variations. The age and sex of the turkey are particularly important in altering the yelp. The deep coarse yelp of an old gobbler will sound very different from the high-pitched yelp of the five-month-old hen. The coarseness of some gobbler yelps is extremely difficult to imitate.

The hunter will also encounter great variations in the volume of yelps. Occasionally a bird will be heard making low, almost contented-sounding yelps. In these cases it appears that the bird is talking to itself. At the other end of the spectrum, the mature hen who is trying to attract her brood will yelp with a volume and persistance that is shocking.

There are many variations in rhythm and the number of notes in a sequence. The effective spring call that hunters refer to as a *cackle* is in fact an extremely fast series of yelps (although most cackles made by turkeys themselves start with a number of sharp clucks that lead into a series of fast yelps). The single-note yelp is a call that is frequently made by turkeys but rarely imitated by hunters who have a tendency to be committed to a specific number of yelps in a series.

The tree yelp is a soft series of muffled yelps that is frequently used by birds as they awake on the roost.

AGE AND SEX DIFFERENCES IDENTIFIABLE
UNDER FIELD CONDITIONS

It is imperative that the hunter learn to identify the sex and age of turkeys under field conditions. In many states, this skill is mandated by law during fall "gobbler-only" seasons. Even in states in which birds of either sex may be legal in the fall, the hunter will need to master the skill to hunt efficiently. During the spring season, the hunter who can estimate the age of a gobbler is also at a distinct advantage.

AGE DISPARITY

The fall hunter's strategy will be dictated by the composition of the flock he scatters. Under normal conditions the flock will either be comprised of hens and their broods of the year or of mature, over-one-year-in-age gobblers. Of the various criteria which can be used to differentiate between these respective types of birds, the most obvious is size. The old gobbler can be more than three times larger than a first-year hen when the fall season opens in October. For most experienced hunters, this size difference allows consistently accurate identification; however, for the novice the challenge is greater. For the inexperienced hunter, all turkeys look large; hence, a seven pound bird is difficult to perceive as small if a twenty-one pound gobbler is not available for comparison. Invariably, when an inexperienced hunter is asked what the birds looked like his response will be, "Well, they looked big."

There is a key that the inexperienced hunter can use to facilitate the process of making an age estimate of birds under the difficult conditions imposed in the field. The key is the morphology of the birds tail. Young birds, hatched the previous spring, will typically have tail feathers which are uneven in length. When the tail is fanned, as it often is in flight, the outer tail feathers will be significantly shorter in length, up to three or four inches shorter, than the middle feathers. The fan thus does not present the even outer contour of the adult bird. This variation is a very useful key to apply when birds are flushed, as the tail will be spread out to help the bird navigate. When I flush a fall flock, the tail is the first key I search for. Especially at long distances, when relative size or morphology of the head and neck becomes difficult to assess, the tail is a useful key.

Even when the bird is not visible, the nature of the calls it makes can be used as a valuable indicator of age. As mentioned above, the whistle and high-pitched yelp are characteristic calls of the young bird. In contrast, the old gobbler will rely on coarse clucks and yelps. The hunter who is aware of these variations can be at a tremendous advantage in developing a realistic strategy with which to deal with the respective types of birds.

In the spring, the differences in the tone and pitch of the gobble can be used to determine the age of the respective gobblers. As will be discussed at length in Chapter Five, concerning spring hunting, determining the age of a gobbler is an important first step to success.

You must be careful about placing too much emphasis on the role of flock structure in determining the age of turkeys; however, when used with care, flock size can be very helpful. In general, large flocks are composed of young birds and small flocks are made up of old gobblers. Before the hunter assumes that the large flock is composed of young birds, he should use as many other types of information as are available to him. As the section on reading sign will indicate in detail, often the droppings, tracks, and scratching of a flock can provide clues to age composition.

Many times such sign can be used to corroborate an impression that flock size gives the hunter.

SEX DISCRIMINATION

Contrary to popular belief, it is not always easy to determine the sex of a bird under field conditions. There is no problem when the bird is in hand or when two birds of opposite sex are together under favorable light conditions; however, the sex of the young bird who is partially screened by brush in poor light will be difficult to establish.

There is a color variation in the feathers of hens and gobblers. Gobblers have black-tipped breast feathers while hen's are brown tipped. Again, when birds of opposite sexes are together in good light the difference is obvious. In poor light the brown cast of the hen's breast can appear very dark. Unfortunately, most observations of the birds, when hunting, is done in modest light.

Perhaps the best key in sexing young birds is the morphology and carry of the head and neck. The young gobbler has a massive and bulbous head. Even when a hen is not available for comparison, the bulbous nature of the gobbler's head will be obvious. Also, the length of the gobbler's legs and his generally more upright posture results in his head being carried higher than a hen's. The hen's head is not nearly as large as the gobbler's and it seems to be a more natural extension of the neck. In addition, feathers extend farther up the neck and head of the hen. In profile, the eye of the gobbler is more than one-half the distance from the lowest edge of the cheek to the top of his head. In the hen, the distance from the bottom of the eye to the edge of the cheek is much less.

Secondary sex characteristics such as the beard and spurs are not valuable keys in sexing immature fall birds under field conditions. The tiny beard will typically be invisible and the spurs will just be small bumps.

The calls of immature fall birds are quite similar, although there are some variations. In general, the young gobbler will be more likely to use the key-key whistle followed by relatively coarse yelps. The young hen will often depend on high-pitched yelps exclusively. As stated, the young gobbler will also gobble in the fall.

The gobble will be discordant and frequently will either be terminated or preceded by a whistle. At times, both hen and gobbler will use the key-key whistle; however, the gobbler is much more apt to terminate the key-key with deep yelps. If a young gobbler does yelp, you should be able to estimate his sex with 98 percent accuracy. The hen with her very high-pitched yelp should be equally easy to sex. Difficulties are encountered when relatively non-diagnostic calls, such as clucks, are used. Under these circumstances, the hunter has to be very careful that he does not become overly confident about his ability to use the calls as a predictor of sex.

· 3 ·

General Hunting Techniques Applicable to Both the Fall and Spring Seasons

The section on communication indicated the wide range of calls made by wild turkeys, as well as the variations in the general calls that are made by birds of different ages and sexes. The challenge presented to the hunter in both the fall and spring is to effectively imitate the correct call at the appropriate time from a logical location.

Making an effective call requires practice; however, it is a skill that can be attained by any hunter.

I will not provide the typical photograph of each type of call. If you don't know what the basic calls look like, which is unlikely, I urge you to open any outdoor magazine, particularly *Turkey Call*, and you will see an example of the types to be discussed.

Most experienced hunters have called birds with many, if not all, of the types of calls. Often a hunter will maintain a specific type of call because of its ability to reproduce one of the sounds turkeys make.

Certain types of calls are often recommended for beginners, as if a general progression through the ranks of call types has to be made. Following this advice I started with a box. If you haven't called before, I suggest you look at the entire range of calls available, listen to the tapes or records made by the men who manufacture them and then make a decision as to the types you want to master. I am a great believer in becoming proficient with more than one type of call. When I hunt, I carry three different types of calls and several varieties of the mouth diaphragm. I suspect that you too will want to experiment with many types of calls. It is true that some people have more trouble mastering certain types of calls than others. In some instances the structure of one's mouth and the dentition you have or do not have may make mouth calls impractical to use. I am reluctant to accept the concept that some elusive lack of musical ability may deprive one of the capacity to operate certain calls. I do not deny that specific individuals may have an innate ability which allows them to master a call more rapidly than others; however, the idea that the lack of musical aptitude will deprive you of the opportunity to master a call is nonsense.

Friction Calls

THE BOX

Perhaps the most popular call currently in use is the wooden box. While size varies, most are about eight inches in length by two inches in width and some three inches deep. The top of the box is hinged at one end so that it can be scraped across the top of either side.

The box can produce fine whines, yelps, and clucks. It is not well suited to imitating the cackle and it is impossible to make the whistling call of the young turkey. Some boxes are designed to be shaken to produce a gobble. I have had gobblers respond to such calls but at best they produce only a fair imitation of the gobble.

From a positive perspective a good box (and only an experienced hunter will be able to tell you if the box you get is a good one) will produce excellent imitations of the raspy yelps of many hens. For most people, the box is the easiest call to master. While I have not observed it, it is probably true that a lucky man or two has called up the first gobbler they heard the morning after they first had a box call in their hands.

On the negative side of the ledger, the box does not have the versatility of many other calls. Regardless of the excellence of the call, most experienced hunters can identify a call made with a box as an imitation. The box has the major disadvantage of being made inoperable in rain, snow, or other conditions in which it becomes wet. Most box calls are bulky and cumbersome. Also, the box call is fragile. Many have been dropped from pockets, or sat upon in blinds. Finally, operation of the box demands significant motion on the part of the hunter. If the turkey is close, the movement of the caller can easily be detected.

THE SLATE CALL

The small slate call has the advantage of being extremely compact. It consists of a small piece of slate, of a variety of shapes but usually circular or rectangular, and a wooden peg used to scratch the slate. Anyone who gets chills at the thought of the sounds made by scraping a slate blackboard will appreciate the basic process by which this sound is made.

The tip of the wooden striker, which is often set in a corn cob or hollow piece of wood to improve the tone, is at times charred. An interesting new design incorporates a plexiglass tip that can be used when wet.

The slate itself should be kept sanded for best results. Sounds are made by pulling the point of the striker across the slate. It is imperative that the slate be held in a cupped hand and against the body, or knee if one is sitting, so that a deep resonance will result. The striker can be pulled in a short straight line across the slate, for a distance of about ¼", or in light circles or loops. These movements will produce sounds which imitate yelps. A wonderful purr can be made by scraping the point across the slate very slowly. A cluck is produced by striking the wooden peg on the slate with a light quick stroke. The whistle-like sounds of young turkeys can be made by repeating several quick long strokes.

I like the slate call. I believe the cluck produced on a fine slate is more realistic than that made on any other type of caller. The purr of the slate is also excellent. The call is at its best with these cluck and purr calls. Despite the hundreds of hours I have spent with my favorite mouth diaphragm calls, I use the slate for clucks and purrs. I always carry it with me. The above comment does not mean that fine yelps cannot be made with the slate. Some of the best yelps I have ever heard were made with a slate and I occasionally use one to imitate a particular tone of yelp.

From my perspective, a good slate produces much more realistic sounds than most box calls.

WINGBONE AND SUCKING CALLS

The wingbone of the adult hen represents one of the oldest of calling devices.

All of these sucking calls are operated in essentially the same fashion. The tube is held between the lips and then air is sucked in with a kind of kissing motion.

These calls are not easy to master; however, they can be used to imitate all calls except the gobble. During the time which I used this type of call exclusively, I had success with both clucks and whistles. The whistle seems to have a tone to which young turkeys are particularly susceptible. I have heard some wonderful yelps made on this type of call, but the ones I produce are not as realistic as those I make on my mouth diaphragms.

If you do not think that you can strengthen the muscles of your lips, the use of this type of call will convince you otherwise.

TUBE, SNUFF, OF PILL-BOX BOX CALLS

The tube or snuff box call consists of a cylindrical tube with a cap in which an aperture, usually of half moon shape, is cut. A rubber diaphragm is stretched over the top so that only a narrow slit exists between the diaphragm and the cap top. The lips are pressed against the diaphragm and air forced through it.

All calls, including the gobble, can be made on the snuff box call. It is particularly effective for making soft feeding and confidence calls. In addition, when operated by an expert it makes the best imitation of the gobble I have ever heard. Calls of this type are relatively compact.

One disadvantage is that, with most calls of this type, skill is needed in learning how to affix and tension the diaphragm. Unfortunately, the diaphragm is not particularly durable and often has to be replaced at the most inconvenient time.

THE MOUTH-HELD DIAPHRAGM CALL

The small, horseshoe-shaped diaphragm call is becoming extremely popular. The compact nature of the call and the realistic sounds which can be made with it are the primary reasons for its deserved popularity.

The call is placed in the mouth with the open end of the horseshoe pointing to the front of the mouth. It is then held against the roof of the mouth with the tongue. Sound is emitted when air is brought over the diaphragm from deep in your chest.

This call can be used to imitate every call the turkey makes. As is the case with many of the tube calls, it is very tough for even the most experienced caller to distinguish between a diaphragm call and a turkey. The fact that most who enter calling contests are using this type of call indicates its effectiveness.

There are many diaphragm calls on the market. They vary tremendously in size, shape, and construction. Basically the call consists of one or more sections of rubber diaphragm stretched across a horseshoe-shaped frame. I have seen frames made of aluminum, lead, plastic, and various metal alloys. Occasionally, tape extends out from the sides of the call. Some calls are flat, while others are concave.

It is imperative that the caller find a call that fits his mouth. Many experienced callers simply cannot use or (in the lexicon of calling culture) run a call that is of a particular shape. As an example, I cannot use a call that has a deep concavity. Friends of mine who are excellent diaphragm callers can't use my calls, which are almost flat.

Diaphragm calls that have two or three separate sections of rubber diaphragm stretched on top of one another have recently become very popular. The tone of these multiple reed calls is excellent.

Good gobbles can be made with the diaphragm call. I have never heard a gobble that was as realistic as that produced on the Morgan tube call, but I have fooled a few birds with the diaphragm gobble.

For most people, it is very difficult to start calling with a diaphragm call. The huffing noises made by beginners are typically very similar. The knack of positioning the call in precisely the right spot and exhaling breath in the correct manner is difficult to acquire. It is even more difficult to teach. I believe the difficulty inherent in teaching the use of the diaphragm is knowing precisely what you do with the shape and position of your mouth and tongue. The most important point to stress is that the caller must persevere with the call. There will come a day when, suddenly, the sound will be made and then adequate yelps will be produced with ease. Many people give up on the diaphragm before they reach this point.

After reasonably good calls are made, the caller should experiment with different types of diaphragms until he finds one that is well suited to his particular style of calling. Often a certain type will provide the best whistle call while another will make the best cluck. Many of us carry different diaphragms with which to make special calls.

Take care of your good diaphragm call. It should be washed off after use and kept in a refrigerator. I learned the last lesson after a call stored in a hunting coat pocket deteriorated after several months. Also, avoid putting a call in your mouth if your mouth still has liquid from certain beverages in it. Ascorbic acid, from vitamin C drinks, can cause problems with the relatively fragile diaphragm. I suspect your favorite soft drink is not the best medium for the diaphragm. Protect your good calls.

GENERAL ADVICE FOR CALLING

Most hunters call too loudly and too often; however, the philosophy of calling once and putting the call away is not the answer. There are times when a number of relatively loud calls is the best strategy. In other circumstances, loud calls will repel a bird. In general, it is wise to assume that loud calls may be detrimental and use them only after the low calls have failed.

THE CLUCK

There are many fine hunters who argue against making use of the cluck because it is so close to the alarm putt of the turkey. It is risky to use the cluck; however, there are times in both the spring and fall when the call is useful. I suggest you learn how to cluck but use the call with discretion, particularly in the spring.

LEARN THE WHISTLE

If you hunt in the fall, you need a good whistle or key-key run. I believe the mouth diaphragm will produce the most realistic whistle. Use this call with confidence in the fall. This is one call with which you can be bold. Interject a spirit of panic into the call and don't worry about high volume! Another advantage of the whistle is that birds do not hear every hunter make this call. Everyone yelps, so birds can become yelp shy.

THE GOBBLE

Learn the gobble well before you use the call when it counts. I suspect that ten birds have been spooked for every one attracted by a gobble call. It can be very productive but there are only a few men who use it regularly with consistent success. If you are new to the game or trying to improve upon the modest success you have had, I suggest you do your gobbling in your living room.

VARIATIONS IN THE YELP

Learn to yelp with different tempo, tone, and pitch. The basic rhythm should be maintained, but you must alter your calls so that it sounds appropriate to birds of varying sexes and ages. The yelp of the old gobbler can be so rough and deep that the novice will wonder if the call is the product of a turkey. This yelp is particularly hard to imitate. In some situations a specific type of call, or a variety of a given type, will provide a deeper tone. Other calls may have a built-in, high-pitched quality.

Alteration in the Pitch and Tone of the Same Mouth Call. The experienced caller can change the pitch and tone of a call by altering the tension of muscles of the throat and changing the pressure with which the diaphragm is held against the roof of his mouth. With practice the same diaphragm can produce calls which range from the high-pitched yelps of the young hen to the much deeper tones of the old gobbler.

IMITATING CONTENTMENT CALLS

Turkeys make many low, light calls when feeding. Purrs, clucks, whines and other sing-song noises are typical. Many very successful hunters never imitate these calls; however, they are an asset to the man who can make them. These calls should be kept very low in volume. I once called two adult gobblers to within sixty yards—after three solid hours of work that saw one bird come over five hundred yards to join the other—only to spook the birds with a purr that was too loud.

CONFIDENCE

The best callers know they call well. Confidence is what separates the fine caller from the average caller and is essential to success. I know men who are literally afraid to call. They are not afraid of being raped by a gobbler but rather they fear failing. Many of these men say they would rather stalk birds. No hunter capable of calling birds to him would prefer to hunt them any other way.

The best fishermen believe each cast will be productive; in a similar manner, the best turkey hunters believe a turkey is ready to come to every call they make. If you lose confidence, you will project your insecurity into your call. I can tell when one friend has given up by the sound of his yelp. If I am capable of hearing that message there is no doubt that Mr. Gobbler will identify the insecurity.

The Danger the Proficient Caller Faces: A man who sounds like a turkey will convince a lot of people a turkey is making his calls. Be prepared to be stalked and called to by others. I hope you will not face the horror of being shot at by the idiots who get access to our woods; however, all good callers should be prepared for the possibility.

There are clues you can use to identify even a good caller who may be trying to work you. Most human callers have a tendency to stay in one place when they call. This is particularly true when they hear a bird calling. Wild turkeys are much more apt to change their locations. Also, most men have a tendency to respond within a fixed period of time to the call of a bird. Turkeys will frequently call while another bird is calling or they will delay their response. Most hunters, even very good ones, will have an established rhythm of response and they will use more yelps than other calls.

In addition, hunters develop a confidence in a particular sequence of yelps. Many hunters I have heard always call with a series of three yelps. Be skeptical of the call that never varies in rhythm or number of notes.

COVER AND CONCEALMENT

As stated above, the eyesight and hearing of the wild turkey are superb. The successful hunter must combat the turkey's ability to hear and see by exercising effective concealment. The point missed by many hunters is that effective concealment cannot be purchased in a sporting goods store. Camouflage clothing is a step toward effective concealment but it alone will not attain the goal. There are many factors more important than camouflage clothing. In fact, effective concealment can be achieved without camouflage clothes. Several excellent hunters I know spurn the idea of camouflage clothing entirely. This does not suggest that they are uninterested in concealment; on the contrary, many hide themselves well.

The prerequisites to effective concealment of the hunter are:

1) Lack of Movement. Regardless of the nature of cover, clothing, or hiding place, a key to avoiding detection by a wild turkey is that the hunter be as motionless as possible. Anyone with even a modest level of experience will recall situations in which his slightest movement resulted in his being detected. The individual who begins to hunt turkeys after hunting other game, particularly whitetail deer, will soon learn that the movements which a deer will not identify will frighten a turkey.

One of the great problems the experienced hunter or guide has with a hunter for whom he is attempting to call a turkey relates to this subject of movement. The inexperienced hunter assumes a blind makes it possible to move. Nothing could be further from the truth. A turkey will see movement within all but the best blinds. Despite the fact that a turkey is capable of detecting the motionless hunter, it is true that frequently a stationary hunter who is well concealed will elude detection; this is particularly likely to occur if the bird itself is moving. As every successful hunter learns, the powers of visual detection are far increased when the searcher is motionless. There is no question that this rule applies to the turkey as well. This is certainly not to suggest that the turkey can't detect motion while moving, but his capabilities are reduced.

The first key is thus, a lack of movement. We are referring to movement of any kind, not just locomotion of the entire body. Few things have saved more turkeys' lives than the hunter's attempt to quickly pull his gun up when a bird suddenly, or finally, comes within range.

2) *Good Personal Camouflage.* There is no question that variations in shade, texture and color help the turkey identify an element in the surroundings that is not natural. As has been known for centuries, color tones can contribute to concealing humans. It is imperative, however, that the hunter understand the advantages which are in fact conferred by camouflage. The donning of a green and brown camouflage pattern hat and jacket is only a modest step toward effective concealment. Many beginning hunters work on the assumption that such garb provides some kind of magical invisibility. Nothing could be further from the truth. Some of the most visible and least well concealed hunters I have seen wore camouflage hats and jackets. A turkey sees the entire hunter. Bright blue jeans, white socks folded back over the tops of boots, shiny hands and face, and the metallic glare from a gun give the turkey all he needs to detect the hunter. Moreover, many types of camoflage clothing patterns, particularly the washed-out light tans and greens, blend in very poorly in many types of natural cover. Camouflage can be an effective vehicle to concealment but only when it is intelligently used.

3) *Camouflage of the Hands and Face.* I would much rather wear a red and black plaid shirt, or a solid green shirt or jacket, with well camouflaged face and hands than a good camouflage jacket without cover for hands and face. If movement has saved more turkeys

than anything else, the glare off hands and face is probably a close second.

4) Lack of Noise. The hunter must not make much noise if he is to avoid detection by the wild turkey. The need for quietness applies to the well camouflaged hunter in a well constructed blind.

It is hard to imagine how much noise the inexperienced or careless hunter can make in a blind. I have hunted with men who coughed, sneezed, belched, and cleared their throats with a consistency and volume that guaranteed no healthy turkey would come within two hundred yards of our position. Another hunter shifted his weight in the blind with such vigor that the noises produced sounded as if he were trying to give away our location. Any unnatural noise that is above the lowest levels of volume will be heard and acted upon by turkeys. These restless hunter noises do carry. One morning the coughing of a hunter three hundred yards from my blind was so loud I found it difficult to believe. If I could hear the coughs distinctly at three hundred yards, at what distance would they warn turkeys of his presence?

The human voice should only be used at the lowest levels possible for communication in the turkey woods. Invariably, I am rude to beginning hunters who will interject "great morning" or, more frequently, "these hills are sure steep," as we walk into the woods. I have now learned to advise people to whisper all the time. The human voice, working at the volume level of normal conversation, carries remarkably well in the woods.

THE BLIND

Many experienced turkey hunters make little attempt to implement personal camouflage. One of the best I have ever hunted with wears a faded army fatigue jacket, khaki pants and laughs at my concealment of hands and face. He is successful because he always calls from an invisible position. Usually he hides in a prone position behind a large log and raises to shoot only when he, with his tremendous experience, has calculated the bird is within range. Despite popular myths to the contrary, no turkey will see through a log. Many men construct heavy blinds that afford all but total protection against detection. This type of blind is fine for the experienced hunter who can calculate where the bird is; however, for the inexperienced the reliance on a formidable blind can cause problems. First, many hunters build large blinds that are themselves conspicuous. One I saw had reflective black vinyl sheets wrapped around it. If the blind were in position for two years the turkeys might accept it, but such a blind would certainly discourage the approach by birds that had not seen it in place the day before. Second, even the blind that fits into the environment well can be so effective in hiding the hunter that he will not be in position to shoot a bird when it is close enough. Often, such blinds will be constructed so that certain zones by which the bird could approach will be screened from the hunter.

A good blind meets the following criteria:

1) It is in a good location.
2) It blends in well with the surroundings.
3) It is easy to shoot out of.
4) It provides concealment from 360 degrees and yet it allows the hunter to take a shot to any of the angles of that 360 degree circle.
5) It should be large enough to allow the hunter[s] to turn and face a bird coming from an unanticipated angle.
6) It should be sturdy in construction so that if you bump a part of it, which the hunter you take with you will do, it will not fall apart.
7) It should be constructed so that hunter movement within it produces as little noise as possible. All leaves and debris should be swept out of the interior.

The accompanying photographs are of blinds that birds were actually killed from. In some cases as many as three different birds were called up to the blinds on successive days.

Of all the points addressed above, the most critical is placing the blind in the right location. The best location is in an area from which turkeys expect another turkey to be calling. This location will, obviously, vary with circumstance. One of the factors which has contributed to the myth of the difficulty implicit in calling turkeys has been that many hunters have made adequate calls from poor locations.

If you are in an area to which turkeys should be easily called—
say a spot from which birds were scattered in the fall or near the
roost of a spring gobbler—the next most important consideration
is the terrain.

THE CONTOUR BLIND

The topography of the ground can be used to make the most
effective of turkey blinds. The contour concept relies on elevations
or depressions to hide the hunter. As an example, one of the best
locations for a blind is in the middle of a relatively broad flat
ridge top. In the sections of Virginia and West Virginia in which I
have hunted, many of these flat ridge tops will be thirty to one
hundred and fifty feet wide. Often the drop-off will be very steep.
If a flock is scattered from or near the ridge top, which will often
be the case as they run to the top of the ridge and then fly off it, I
build a blind in the middle of the flat ridge. As map number one
shows, the bird that comes in will only be visible at a range of
from fifteen to seventy-five feet, depending on the width of the
ridge (the distance from X to A or X to B). *More importantly,* I will
only be visible to the bird at that distance as well. If you do what
most beginners do and build the blind at either A or B, so that
you can see the bird approach, the blind will be visible to the bird
for the distance C to A. This distance could be as much as several
hundred yards if the slope is gentle and the area is relatively open.

The contour concept can also be used in a bottom area, as de-
picted on the map. In this case, the depression hides the hunter
until the birds are within range.

The use of these blinds has resulted in many of the hunters I
have guided killing birds at ranges of only ten to twenty-five
paces. Probably because of the size of our ridge tops, a number of
kills have been at twenty paces.

The advantages of the contour blind concept are many. Of the
greatest significance is the fact that the bird simply cannot see
you until it is within range. Despite the advantage of the contour,
I am not suggesting you stand in the middle of the ridge in anticipation of the bird popping his head over the contour. Unless you
are very quick, or lucky, with the shot you will simply be a witness

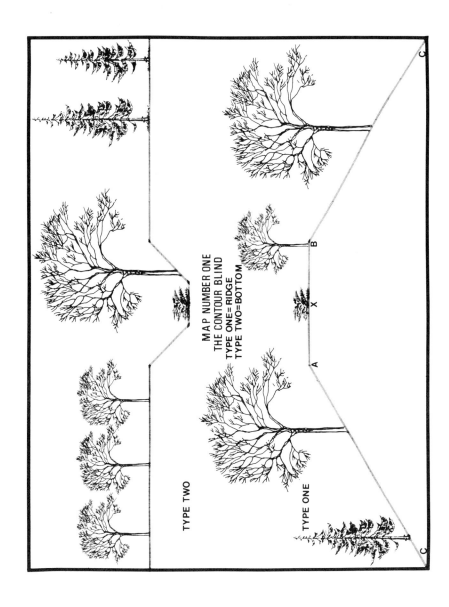

MAP NUMBER ONE
THE CONTOUR BLIND
TYPE ONE = RIDGE
TYPE TWO = BOTTOM

TYPE TWO

TYPE ONE

to nature's greatest disappearing act. A blind at point X is a good idea. Another advantage of the contour cover is that it can offset a lot of errors by hunters in the blind. Movement in the blind and some noises are not as likely to be picked up by the bird, because the contour not only keeps the bird from seeing movement but also reduces the ease with which sound waves reach him.

Interestingly, turkeys do not seem to be particularly suspicious about sticking their heads up over the contour. Almost invariably their reaction will be to stop to assess their new perspective. The alert pause affords the opportunity for an accurate shot.

An increasingly important advantage of the contour blind is that it decreases the chances of another hunter shooting into your blind. The other hunter, just like the turkey you are trying to call, does not have a direct line of sight to your blind. It is disturbing that you must be concerned about calling up other hunters, but in most areas it has become a serious problem. It seems incredible that anyone could be so stupid and blatantly irresponsible as to shoot at the sound of a turkey, but it has happened. In some areas, the contour blind and highly visible clothing may be the best protection against this unnecessary horror. I have enjoyed the luxury of hunting relatively wild areas, but the reports from my friends in areas which receive heavy hunting pressure are chilling. If you hunt in an area in which you anticipate intense hunting pressure, I suggest you wear orange, use the contour blind concept and accept the disadvantages that your visibility will afford in some situations.

If someone tells you it is impossible to call up birds while wearing colorful clothing, he is either limited in experience or hasn't exercised any intelligence in compensating for the visibility of the clothes. It can be done. Regardless of the area I hunt, I always carry a bright orange day pack on my back. Where I am comfortable in terms of the lack of hunting pressure and the general remoteness of the area, I will sit on the pack or hide it in my blind. When walking in and out of the woods, the visible orange pack is always on my back.

During the fall season, I have walked right into flocks of turkeys with the orange pack on my back. In the spring, I have called up mature gobblers with it on my back when caught in relatively open areas. There is a need to recognize that today, in most areas, irresponsible people have access to you; moreover, the situation will probably become more dangerous in the future.

BEHAVIOR IN THE BLIND

Let me watch a hunter sit in a blind and I will tell you what his level of experience is. The experienced hunter will anticipate the arrival of the bird. All the movements he makes will have a purpose. The inexperienced hunter is inevitably unprepared for the arrival of the turkey. Also he will shift his position as the bird approaches. In over 95 percent of situations the hunter should be able to hear a bird walking towards him. Often the angle of the bird's approach will also be indicated by the bird's calls. The hunter should have his gun raised and pointed at the spot from which he expects the bird to come over the contour. The hunter's face should be on the comb of the stock. The safety of the gun should be off and he should be ready to shoot.

When a turkey sticks his head up over a ridge, the only move I want to make is with my right index finger. If your hearing is good, you should be able to predict with precision the point at which the bird will appear. You should have your blind constructed so that the barrel rests on a part of the blind and is aimed at the precise point at which you expect the bird to arrive. It is not difficult to do this; I have done it many times. It is interesting to see how hard it is for inexperienced hunters to predict the spot from which the bird will appear. In 95 percent of the times I have called birds to hunters for the first time, despite my detailed instructions, there will be a flurry of movement when the turkey's head appears. Some movement will be a result of nervousness, but most is based on the hunter's inability to anticipate where the bird will arrive. The hunters think they are looking at the right spot but are not. You must be ready. A turkey will not allow you much adjustment. If you, or a hunter with you, jerks his head down to the rib of his gun the bird will explode into flight. In most cases, he will become airborne by whirling around and propelling himself down the slope. Such a target is a tough one for the coolest and most experienced of hunters.

CALLING WITHOUT A BLIND

Sometimes you do not have time to build a blind before you call. I find this is much more likely to occur in the spring season than in the fall. In the spring, one must react quickly to the location of a gobbler. Also, a fine spring tactic is to move as you call. There is no time to build a blind under such circumstances; in contrast, in the fall one can usually build a blind at leisure after the birds have been scattered. For these reasons, I believe it is more important to have complete personal camouflage in the spring than in the fall.

When searching for birds in either the fall or the spring, one should take the time to get in a well hidden position before calling. Often I have failed to do this, usually because fatigue and a lack of sign have convinced me that the birds are not in the immediate area. Many times I have paid for my lack of care by having a bird pop into range and dart away as it saw me. Try to muster the discipline to hide well before you call. Frequently, the effort will go for naught; however, the day will come when a fine gobbler will be your just reward.

READING SIGN

The hunter must learn to read turkey sign effectively if he is to find birds consistently. Several types of sign offer valuable clues to when, how many, and what types of birds were in a specific area.

SCRATCHING

Turkeys characteristically rake debris from the forest floor in searching for many types of food. The sign left by this process is known as scratching. The birds will rake a ten-to-twelve-inch diameter circle clean of leaves with several strokes of their feet. The bird will stay in essentially the same position as he rakes, hence the debris is normally deposited behind him. At times, toe prints will be visible in the moist soil under the leaves. The scratching is inevitably much more regular in appearance than that produced by deer as they paw the leaves in their search for mast. Often the deposition of leaves and the shape of the scratched area can provide clues to the direction taken by a bird or birds; however, birds will also wander around as they scratch, which makes determining the direction of movement difficult.

If a good-size flock has spent time in a rich food area, the extent of the scratching can be shocking. Often an entire hillside or small basin will seem to be totally covered with scratching. Such areas can often be identified from a considerable distance by the hunter. In fact, the intelligent use of a good pair of binoculars will allow the hunter to locate areas that have been heavily scratched at remarkable distances.

The hunter must not only learn to identify scratching but must also be capable of determining it age. Fresh scratching will typically be clear of leaves or other debris that will accumulate within it with time. The exposed dirt will be moist and dark before it dries out through exposure to the sun. At times, the marks made by the toes will be sharp and well defined. Leaves that have been raked to the rear will still be moist on the side that was next to the ground. Also, dirt thrown to the rear during the scratching will be on top of leaves.

It is a challenge to differentiate two-day-old from three-day-old scratchings. Here the clues that allow the identification of fresh scratching are gone and the hunter must rely on relative age. The challenge is exacerbated by the effects of weather. Scratching will look older quicker under certain weather conditions. Experience is the key to making accurate estimates. Whenever you have the opportunity to hunt consecutive days in an area in which you have found fresh sign, you should make the effort to see what the scratching looks like on each successive day. The lessons learned by such an exercise will prove valuable.

The amount of scratching in an area can be used to obtain a rough estimate of the size of the group of turkeys. One problem which obviates the ability to develop a formula for converting the number of scratchings to the number of turkeys is that it is impossible to know precisely how much time the birds spent in searching for food. A small group of turkeys that spent a long time in a given area may produce as much sign as a large drove which used the area only briefly. In general, the amount of fresh scratching can be used to gain a fair estimate of flock size. In most cases, the relationship is such that small flocks of old gobblers can be distinguished from large droves of young birds and their mothers.

DROPPINGS

Diet, health and weather conditions all play a role in determining the shape and structure of turkey droppings; however, some variations are related exclusively to the age and sex of the bird.

Male droppings are normally straight in shape with a small hook at the end of the stool. Hen droppings are normally deposited in a spiral shaped mass. These sex variations hold up with normal diets.

A careful inspection of the droppings can allow the hunter to estimate their age. Very fresh droppings are warm and moist. As time passes, the dropping will cool off, dry out, an become much firmer in texture. The degree of dryness of the stool allows an estimate to be made of its age. Droppings that are dry on the outside but still moist inside are probably two or three days old. Droppings that are dry throughout but which still maintain their shape are about a week old. Those droppings that are older than a week will begin to lose their shape.

Even old droppings can be useful in locating a popular roosting area. Areas under frequently used roosts will be covered with droppings.

TRACKS

In some types of terrain, tracks constitute an important type of sign. The size of the turkey and the shape of his foot assure that discernible tracks will be made in a variety of environments.

The problems inherent in determining the age of tracks of most species of game are applicable to turkeys. In general, a fresh track will be clean, sharp and well defined. A track that is over a day old will begin to lose its sharp edges and often will collect debris. In snow, a track's age is easier to establish because the deterioration in the sharpness of the track occurs more rapidly. Regardless of the medium in which the track is deposited, the hunter needs to develop the skill of determining its age. As mentioned before with respect to scratching, it is wise to return to tracks to see how they are altered with time.

The size of the footprint of the wild turkey can be used to estimate the sex of the bird that made it. In most instances, mature gobbler tracks will be in excess of 4¼ inches in length when measured from the tip of the middle toe to the heel. Hens, and immature gobblers in their first fall, will measure under 4¼ inches in length. The size and thickness of the print and the distance between the individual prints can be used by the hunter to estimate the bird's size and age. In spring, the tracks of the gobbler take on an unusual appearance when made during the strut. The tracks will be placed close together, and the turns and alterations that the bird makes during the mating ritual will also be decipherable. In addition, evidence of dragging tips of the primary feathers often will be found. The marks made by the wings will be straight lines parallel to and outside the footprints.

FINDING TRACKS

Many types of terrain are not conducive to the recording of tracks. No tracker is so skilled at reading sign that he is able to read tracks made on rocks. Many types of dense, low vegetation also make it unlikely that tracks will be left. In contrast, old roads and areas around springs, ponds and streams are particularly good areas in which to find tracks. Any ground cover that is moist and relatively free of vegetation will take and hold tracks.

DUSTING AREAS

Turkeys will dig shallow depressions in sand or loose dirt for the purpose of dusting themselves. Old road beds and sandy banks along streams are likely areas in which the birds will wallow. Frequently, feathers from the birds can be found in these shallow, dish-shaped depressions.

The age of dusting areas can be estimated using the same techniques that the hunter develops to assess the age of scratching.

FEATHERS

Healthy turkeys will frequently drop feathers as they feed, dust, or simply walk or fly.

The intelligent hunter should look for feathers as he hunts. While scouting, the hunter can determine if turkeys have used a field for feeding on grasshoppers by the location of feathers. In many fields, the close-cropped grass makes the discovery of other types of sign—such as droppings, scratching, or tracks—unlikely.

Feathers are durable, so the hunter must learn to determine the age of a feather before he becomes too excited about finding it. Feathers become quite dirty and weathered looking with age, and with a little experience the hunter can differentiate between recently lost feathers and those of considerable age.

SHOFFSTALL

· 4 ·

The Fall

The popularity of spring turkey hunting has increased dramatically in recent years. Most of us who hunt turkeys enjoy the spring season tremendously; however, I am afraid this interest has resulted in hunters overlooking the opportunities available in the fall.

For the individual who wants to enjoy an introduction to turkey hunting, the fall provides significant advantages. Of primary importance is that this period offers an opportunity to harvest young birds. For the beginner or the relatively inexperienced hunter, the young bird's behavior is more predictable than that of mature spring gobblers.

Numerous articles and sections of books have outlined the basic steps to successful fall turkey hunting. These principles are:
1) Find a flock of hens and their young of the year;
2) Scatter the flock;
3) Call up the young birds.

The first step—finding a flock—is the most difficult. A key which will increase your odds is to plan your hunting time so that you hunt as many consecutive days as possible. Assuming that you are in good turkey country, the chances of finding a flock are increased immeasurably if you can spend a number of consecutive days searching for sign. These days allow you to eliminate those areas which the birds are not using. In contrast, if you decide to hunt on five separate days during the season, the decision not to investigate an area that was not being used on your previous hunt is foolish. The glade that was not used two weeks ago may now be where the turkeys are. Another advantage of consecutive hunting days is that they allow the hunter to return to a spot where he scattered birds the day before. Despite many reports to the contrary, even birds scattered before noon will often wait until the next day to regroup. If you are due back on the job the next day, it will not be too reassuring to realize that you still have five days to hunt later in the season.

A second key factor contributing to the ease with which a hunter can find fall turkeys is for him to cooperate with a friend. To find flocks of turkeys consistently, one must cover many acres. Two men can cover twice the area that one can. A friend of mine and I invariably hunt in different areas. If one of us encounters birds, or fresh sign, we exchange the information in the evening and the next day cooperate in an intensive hunt. This technique more than doubles our chances of encountering fall flocks. The lone hunter, frustrated by a failure to find a flock, will often become discouraged. The hunter who knows his friend is investing a similar effort is more likely to work hard in his own zone of responsibility.

Annual Variations in Range of Fall Flocks

The fall hunter must locate the areas in which turkeys are feeding each year. The compact covers used by grouse, woodcock, and pheasant may be productive year after year, but turkey cover use is not so easy to predict. The grape thicket that was consistently used by turkeys last year may never be used this fall. The critical factor determining which covers will be productive is the productivity of food sources within them. During years in which acorn production is minimal but the greenbrier crop is good, the birds will be found exclusively in the greenbrier covers. In a year in which the corn is plentiful, the birds will be among the large oaks.

When the mast crop of oak is excellent the birds will be particularly difficult to find because there is so much food in so many areas. The years in which a major mast crop, such as oak, is very poor will, conversely, be times when the birds are easier to find. The ease of finding the birds in these periods is based on the restricted availability of secondary food sources.

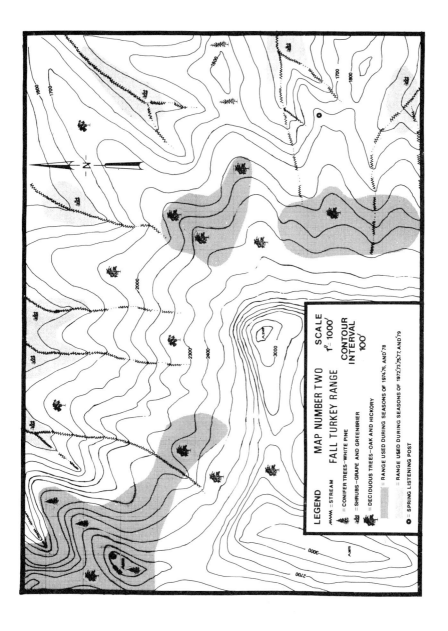

Many fall hunters who have failed to learn the varied ranging practices of turkeys have often erroneously assumed that "there are no birds this year." Frequently this means only that the birds are not using the areas in which the hunter found them last year. They may be and often are present in large numbers in other covers.

Map number two shows a typical section of mountainous turkey range. The areas that are cross-hatched were the zones primarily used by turkeys in specific fall seasons. In other falls, the birds were in the sections that are shaded. The shaded area comprises mature hardwoods—primarily hickory and oak. The cross-hatched zone is a cut-over area in which grape, greenbrier, paw-paw, and dogwood are prevalent.

The maps demonstrate that the hunter who found turkeys in the grape must learn they will not be there every fall. They may, of course, be in such cover for three falls in a row, but on the fourth they may not. It is interesting to note that when the birds are in the hardwood cover they are much harder to find. The years they are in the hardwoods, they stay in certain bands despite the fact the good oak mast is everywhere. In this case, the birds enjoy the luxury of picking the best territory for reasons other than food production. Hence, the hunter has to search all the areas in which ample oak mast exists. This large area is difficult to cover. The turkeys are not so fortunate in a poor acorn year. In these years they will be in the few areas which produce the grape, greenbrier, or paw-paw. In one such year, we found birds in a specific cover every time we hunted it.

The experienced hunter can anticipate where the birds will be from the food crop. It is true that a flock will always be somewhere within a general range; however, unless you can restrict the zone you will be a very tired and frustrated hunter. It is narrowing the feeding areas down that helps separate the successful turkey hunters from the rest.

THE TURKEY DOG

One argument frequently directed against the wild turkey is that since it can't be hunted with dogs it does not deserve the title of king of the uplands. The turkey can and often has been effectively hunted by dogs during the fall season. The dog must be intelligent and obedient. The strategy employed is to allow the dog to search for a flock of birds which he will scatter. The hunter then calls the dog to him and the dog and his master wait in silent ambush at the point from which the birds scattered. The dog must remain motionless and hidden during the time-consuming process of calling the scattered birds back. Anyone who has trained a dog with the hunting desire necessary to go out and find turkeys in big country can imagine the challenge involved in maintaining control over the dog when it returns to the blind. The art of hunting turkeys with dogs is not a popular one because of the difficulties involved in training the dog; however, the dog can be an effective companion for the turkey hunter who is willing to work even harder than one must to develop an efficient pointing dog. No turkey dog has ever been called a field champion. I suspect few of the great ones are registered dogs. The praises of the accomplished turkey dog are sung in hardware stores in hot southern towns, places where men who know dogs meet and talk.

My own partner and I have become great believers in the advantages of using a dog to find fall turkeys. We have learned that the dog does not have to be a superbly well trained turkey dog; however, he must respond to the hunter and resist the temptation to chase game other than turkeys. My grouse dogs, Brittany Spaniels, work very well as turkey finders. The enjoyment they derive from scattering a flock of turkeys in no way has detracted from their grouse performances. On several occasions, it has been during successful grouse hunts that the dogs have encountered flocks of turkeys. The dogs will not only increase the number of flocks found, but they scatter the birds more effectively. The key again is not to *scare* a flock but to *scatter* it. If the birds fly off together, they will not need to get back together, and the opportunity to call the separated birds is lost. A dog all but assures the effective dispersion of any flock you encounter. Since my dogs are not trained to lie in the blind without moving, after the birds have been scattered, I take them back to the car before returning to call the turkeys. In most instances, my return takes place early the next morning; however, if I do scatter birds in the morning, I can usually be back in the blind within an hour.

TAKING ADVANTAGE OF WEATHER IN FINDING THE DROVE—SNOW

Fall turkeys are much easier to find when snow is on the ground. If you are lucky enough to be able to hunt at short notice, there is no better situation to take advantage of than snow. Last year on three occasions we used the snow to help us find turkeys. The fact that turkeys must feed during the day means that the speed with which a flock travels is not too great. The persistent hunter will usually find a flock within an hour or two of taking up a fresh trail. In many instances, when the flock is encountered they will flush within shotgun range. The ability to get close is of course dependent on the nature of the terrain and cover and the size and composition of the flock. A fresh snow also provides a tremendous advantage for the hunter in recovering crippled birds. Last year, one of my friends attributed his success in running down a crippled bird primarily to the sign left behind in the snow. Always take advantage of the snow!

SCATTERED!

Once the birds have been found and scattered, the hunter faces the challenge of calling the birds back to him. The first step to success at this stage of the hunt is the intelligent location of your blind. If you use a fair call from the correct position, your chances of killing a fall turkey are high. If you use an excellent call from a bad position, your chances are poor. The blind should be near the spot from which the birds are flushed. It is often true that if it is slightly uphill, it will work perfectly, but I have made the error of placing a blind too far above the flushing spot only to watch the birds regroup below me. A good rule is to locate the blind precisely where they flushed.

As indicated in the section of calls, the whistling kee-kee run will often bring young turkeys on the run. The young hen will usually be much easier to call than the young gobbler. In many cases, hens will come to the first few calls you make. Do not be bashful about making enough calls. A young turkey expects another lost bird to be eager to regroup.

If you have a bird coming to your call, don't feel that you must take the first opportunity for a shot. As long as he comes with confidence, let him come. There is no need to shoot at forty yards or even thirty. If he is young and fooled, he will come to within the optimum twenty-yard range.

There are two major threats to the successful implementation of this simple fall strategy. First, the flock you scatter may not consist of young turkeys but rather old gobblers. In this case, the birds will not respond to the same calls. In addition, the old birds are far more difficult to call even when you effectively imitate their coarse yelps and deep clucks.

If you do scatter a flock of old gobblers, I suggest you follow the steps outlined above with two critical exceptions. First, you must make calls that old gobblers expect their friends to make. Second, you must be prepared to wait longer because they will take longer to regroup. Mature gobblers are very tough to fool in the fall.

If the flock is large, it is highly probable that it is composed of hens and their young. These flocks will vary in size but most I find average about ten to twelve birds. That may be less than the flock size described in the literature, but that is what I have encountered.

When a flock of hens and young birds is scattered, a major threat to the strategy we have discussed is the old hen herself. As you call you may find you are competing, unsuccessfully, with the hen in an attempt to attract the birds. The old hen will establish a regrouping spot near the point at which the flock was dispersed and begin to yelp incessantly as she calls her brood. Do not try to compete with the hen; rather, flush the hen and chase her from the area. If you fail to chase the hen, all the young birds will go to her.

Do not give up if you call a young bird up and miss it. Young turkeys will often come to a blind after another bird has been shot at. Just last season there were two occasions when I called several birds up from the same flush. On one occasion, a third bird, a young hen, was called after two birds had come and been shot at and missed. The sound of a shot does not terrify a turkey. The human voice will not be tolerated but the report of the gun, even at close range, must sound like crashing trees or thunder to the bird and is not inherently frightening. I have noticed that birds that come after a shot has been missed are usually silent. The third bird that came to our blind on that one incredible morning did not make a sound.

SPLINTER FLOCKS IN THE FALL

Under normal hunting pressure, large groups of turkeys composed of several hens and their respective broods will rarely stay together for the entire fall season. Sometimes fission of fall flocks will occur for reasons other than hunting pressure; however, in most cases it is repeated scattering by hunters and their dogs that splits large droves into smaller flocks. These splinter flocks will vary in size from a pair to six or seven birds.

Hunters often make the mistake of assuming that a splinter flock is made up of the survivors of the original droves encountered in the same area during the late summer or early fall. Certainly some attrition will have taken place by the time the splinter flocks are formed, but in most cases there are many more hens and their young than are represented by a single splinter flock. The rest of the original drove has simply split off and established a separate range. There are times when these splinter elements will come into contact with one another and a process of recombinations will occur. This is particularly likely to occur in periods of reduced hunting pressure following heavy hunting, for example, after a week of deer hunting.

Many inexperienced hunters make the mistake of assuming that any flock of less than ten birds is composed of old gobblers. In areas subjected to heavy hunting pressure, it is just as likely that a flock of six birds will be a splinter group of a hen and her young.

Large droves of hens and their young will occasionally be encountered late in the fall season. When this does occur, it is highly likely that the hunter is in an area that has received relatively modest hunting pressure.

Members of small splinter flocks are particularly susceptible to calling. One factor that influences this susceptibility is that in most cases the adult hen will not be a member of the flock. When the few young birds are scattered, they are very eager to get back together and they expect to hear, and will respond quickly to, the calls of other young birds. I have had members of these splinter flocks come running directly to the blind at the first calls I made.

Mixed Fall Flocks

Occasionally, a group of birds consisting of both hens with their young and old gobblers will be encountered. This is likely to occur during years in which food is available only in restricted areas. In such situations the integrity of the respective flocks is not lost; what the hunter has encountered is a situation in which necessity has brought the respective flocks together. The situation can be confusing to the hunter attempting to interpret the composition of the group of birds. The error that most hunters make is to assume that the entire group of birds is a single flock. The birds encountered will in fact be members of two or more distinct flocks. In such a situation, the hunter will often succeed in scattering only one of the flocks—the other flock will run off in great alarm but will not be scattered. If only the gobblers have been scattered and the hunter tries to attract the birds back using the lost calls of young birds, he will fail. Many hunters have no doubt made such a mistake in flock identification and never been aware of it. This probably explains what occurs on those instances when part of a large flock is scattered late in the afternoon and the next morning the hunter gets no response to his normally deadly key-key calls.

It is essential that the fall hunter make a rapid and accurate identification of the flock. A failure to accomplish this will jeopardize the rest of his effort regardless of the skill with which he implements his subsequent techniques.

] 67 [

HUNTING PRESSURE IN THE FALL

I can't imagine a situation in which a spring hunter enjoys the idea of unknown hunters being in the area he has chosen to hunt. In the fall, many successful hunters suggest the more hunters the merrier. This is because turkeys must be located and scattered in the fall to be susceptible to calling. The hunter who enjoys company is suggesting that said company will help keep the birds scattered and susceptible to being called.

As mentioned above, a group of hunters working together can be a great advantage in attempting to find turkeys in big country; however, most experienced hunters would agree that too much pressure can also cause problems in the fall.

In many states, the first week of the fall deer season runs concurrently with the turkey season. The great hunting pressure exerted during the deer season will often alter turkey behavior. One reaction is a decline in calling by birds of all ages and sexes. Also, the larger flocks of several hens and their young of the year will fission to form the small splinter flocks. Under intense pressure, some birds, even young ones, will simply refrain from trying to get back with the flock and adopt a solitary existence. Often this period of isolation will be terminated only when the bird sees other turkeys and they regroup by sight alone.

It has been my experience that the turkey hunting is good during the first few days of the deer season, in fact it may be excellent because of the number of birds that are separated; however, by the end of the first week the turkeys are reluctant to answer calls and will stay hidden until the pressure passes. There is no question that the hunting improves markedly several days after the deer season closes. Turkeys will gradually drift back together to form larger groups and calling will become more frequent.

My studies indicate that the range of birds is also restricted during these periods of intense pressure. Several days after the deer season closes the areas in which there is heavy scratching will increase in size and accessible zones, used in the beginning of the season, will begin to be worked again.

CALLING BIRDS YOU HAVE NOT SCATTERED

Most of one's energy in the fall is expended in searching for flocks; however, the intelligent hunter will understand that birds may have been scattered by other hunters, or other predators, and be susceptible to calling. Experienced hunters will periodically call while hunting. An intelligent balance must be maintained between calling too much and, hence, reducing your chances of finding the flock, and not waiting in one spot long enough for a separated bird to respond. Many opportunities to kill birds are lost because hunters are not patient after making their calls.

Occasionally, the hunter can guess that birds may have been scattered in a given area and go there on the assumption they will be susceptible to his calls. For example, suppose there is an area that you know is hunted exclusively by a few avid deer hunters. Prior to the deer season you notice a lot of turkey sign in this area. After the first day or two of the deer season you may suspect that some of the young birds will have been scattered and might still be isolated. If you are clever, you might select the right spot from which to call.

Last fall, with a guest from four hundred miles away, I made the right choice and a nice young gobbler came at least three hundred yards to my calls. In this case, I correctly suspected that the birds had probably been scattered in the area and that the deer hunters had not called to them.

You will experience times when your calling will be unproductive. In fact, the challenge of calling before you have scattered birds is to have the discipline and confidence to believe the birds will come. If you lose confidence, you will not be prepared for the bird that does decide to come.

THE FALL CHALLENGE—GOBBLERS ONLY
(*If you are good enough.*)

If fall turkey hunting is legal, the hunter should be allowed to kill hens as well as gobblers. To place a legal restraint on hens is to put many honorable hunters in the position of being game law violators because they failed the difficult challenge of distinguishing between a young hen and a young gobbler. Under hunting conditions, even the most experienced hunters can make mistakes in sexing young birds. The young hunter who calls a bird up should have the right to kill it cleanly.

However, if you are good enough, you should adopt a policy of shooting only gobblers. With experience, and patience, you can learn to eliminate the mistakes in identification. The policy will result in your passing up many young hens that come running to your calls. There may be long stretches when you are convinced that there are only young hens in your area. Patience will prove you wrong. The gobbler will come—and when he does the satisfaction will be compounded by the knowledge that you let a number of strong young hens pass and hopefully survive to breed and raise young gobblers and hens themselves.

This challenge is too great for the young or inexperienced hunter to meet. All of us have been in those categories and many of us killed our first fall turkeys with little thought of their gender. They were *turkeys* and we couldn't wait to run home with them.

When you feel you are good enough, try to harvest only gobblers. You need not wear a badge attesting to your policy but I submit it would be a good idea to support the concept publicly. When people begin to ask you to take them out, as they will if you work at the sport, make them adopt your policy. Perhaps not on the first bird you call up for a friend, but after they have had that first bird try to convince them of the value and the pride that is derived from killing gobblers only.

Make no mistake about it, the policy is a tough one. Young gobblers are much more difficult to kill than young hens. The great pride will come in responding to someone who rushes to your car holding an eight-pound hen and screams, "Got yours yet, John?" you can simply say, "No, not yet." As you drive away, you can smile with the knowledge that you have passed up five young hens you had within twenty feet. Such a tactic is not designed to gain status in the local barber shop. It will, however, do wonders for your self-esteem as you sit in a barber shop and listen to the stories.

This section does not intend to suggest that the popularity of the spring season is unjustified. On the contrary, all of us who love turkeys enjoy the thrills of the spring; however, do not relegate your hunting of turkeys to the spring alone. The turkey provides great sport in the fall as well. The thrill of a new snow and the knowledge that you will probably find the flock somewhere on the mountain the next day is intoxicating. In addition, the rooting of a gobbler in the spring is not nearly as sure a thing as busting up a flock late on a fall afternoon.

COMMON ERRORS OF THE FALL HUNTER:

1) A failure to develop a specific strategy for finding fall flocks jeopardizes the success of many hunters. Haphazard wandering through even excellent turkey range will prove frustrating. The hunter must diligently search areas that are being used by turkeys.

2) Many hunters make the mistake of assuming the birds will be where they were in a previous fall. The experienced hunter learns that this is a mistake. Each year an effort must be made to locate areas which are currently productive.

3) The inexperienced hunter often assumes that a good call will attract turkeys from any location, and at any time. Even the best call will only be effective if it is made from a logical location and at the right time. This mistake of attributing to turkeys a vulnerability to any realistic sounding call is one of the major errors which undermines the success of many fall hunters. Fall turkeys, particularly young ones, are vulnerable only to the right call from the right location. If birds have not been scattered, it is rare that they will come to any call, regardless of its quality.

4) A failure to scatter a fall flock is another mistake commonly committed. The hunter may find a flock and attempt to scatter it; however, if dispersion of the birds is not accomplished, the hunter's calling will be unproductive. Many flocks that are flushed by hunters are not scattered. Birds may run or fly off together.

5) The hunter who has mastered only one call, a yelp, is operating at a serious disadvantage. The error of depending on

the yelp is easy to make, as it will attract some birds; the key-key whistle, however, is a better fall call and every serious hunter should use it. The number of young fall birds you call will increase significantly after you have mastered the key-key call.

6) A error that is often made by the hunter who has enjoyed great success with the key-key whistle is to depend on it exclusively. If old gobblers are scattered, the hunter must alter his calling. A gobbler does not expect his comrades to be making young turkey calls and he will not be attracted to such calls even if he is convinced the call is being made by another turkey. He, the old gobbler, has no reason to seek out the company of a young turkey.

7) Many hunters have lost the opportunity to call up a young bird by attempting to compete with the old hen as she called the brood back to her. If the old hen begins to call, the hunter must leave his blind and flush her from the area. No caller can compete with the hen. The act of reflushing the hen will not significantly reduce one's chances to call the young birds.

8) Many hunters, often some with considerable experience, make the error of failing to try to call up additional birds after one has been shot at. As previously mentioned, more than one young bird can be called to the same blind. I have called five different young birds to the same blind on the same day. Also, if a large flock is scattered early in the season it is not unusual for the hunter to call birds back to the same blind on several mornings in a row. Do not make the mistake of assuming that missing one bird has ruined your chances to take advantage of a well scattered flock of young birds.

9) The fall hunter will make a serious error if he does not persevere in the blind. Often inexperienced hunters will not wait long enough to allow birds to come to their calling. If old gobblers have been scattered, the hunter should be prepared to endure a long wait. Many old gobblers have enjoyed great longevity because they were very slow in regrouping after being scattered. Patience is a necessary attribute to the successful fall hunter.

10) A mistake that many first-time hunters make is shooting at a bird before it is close enough to the blind. If a young bird is fooled, it will come right to the caller. There is no need to shoot

the instant it is within fifty yards. There are few errors which save as many turkeys as premature shooting. Let the bird get close. A lot of turkeys have been crippled at forty yards. Twenty yards is a much more lethal range.

11) A failure to identify the composition of the flock that has been scattered is another mistake that has cost fall hunters many birds. The hunter must learn how to identify young from old birds at various ranges and under varying light conditions.

A Successful Fall Hunt—

The dark hills are silhouetted against the slightly lighter sky as I pull onto the logging road. This leg of the trip is rough, and I brace myself in the seat as the bouncing headlights cut through the trees. Finally, I reach the area from which the hunt will begin. Stepping from the jeep, I am greeted by the cool air of the mountain. I close the door of the big vehicle with care. I hate the loud, metallic sounds the latch produces. Despite the lack of light, I am comfortable and relaxed as I set out on the familiar trail. My clothes fit perfectly, the gun is familiar, and the boots have logged one hundred miles on this mountain. The smells of the November woods, the strength of my body, and the expectations of the day surge through me. Damn, it's great to be on the mountain!

I walk through the dark woods towards the big hardwoods near the head of the little cove. I saw fresh sign in the area two days before, and if I am lucky. . . . As dawn comes, I listen for the sounds of birds leaving their roosts. No such sounds are forthcoming. I begin the arduous search for the flock. There are no shortcuts. I go up and over ridges, and down into basins, and along small streams. I discipline myself to approach each ridge with caution and to search each cove with the bright binoculars. My legs begin to ache, and despite the forty-degree temperature, sweat rolls down my face. I have hunted hard and am satisfied with the morning.

There is not time for the grouse hunter's relaxed lunch on the tailgate of a station wagon. There is no time to play with the warm and happy Brittany after lunch. The turkey hunter opens his meager lunch on a high, hardwood ridge overlooking a spring.

You are still turkey hunting. You need every minute, every day, if you want to be able to kill them with the consistency that separates the turkey hunter from the good old boy who blundered into them.

After lunch, I plan the hunt for the afternoon. It is warmer. I decide to work down along an ample stream that drains the large mountain to my north. It is almost three when I finally reach the valley. I bend to drink from the small stream, confident that there is no threat of pollution here, back from the roads, the cattle, the quail, and the quail hunters. Drinking from clear streams is one of the fringe benefits of turkey hunting. After a brief pause, I continue to hunt.

The small circle of earth, devoid of leaves, sends a shiver through my body. My entire body tightens as I inspect the sign—fresh! The scratching indicates a large flock. I move quickly, aware that the birds may be within one hundred yards. My body drinks the adrenalin and I acquire new strength. Turkeys! I pause and hear them raking the leaves in front of me. There is no question about the rhythmic sound the large birds make as they scratch in the cluttered forest floor in search of mast. I judge them to be seventy-five to one hundred yards downstream. I move carefully. The knowledge that I will get close to them increases the thrill. The laurel opens a bit, and I see them. Several of the sleek, great birds are by the bank of the stream. My mind races as I assess the situation. Am I close enough to rush? Would it be better to try to circle in front of the feeding flock? Have they sensed my presence? The quick putt-putt alarm call answers my question.

I throw myself toward them. The sprint is the infantryman's rush, hampered by equipment, the mobility of the arms restricted by the heavy gun. I rushed this way once, not long ago, carrying an M16. There was no more effort expended than there is now. The birds lift their heads quickly. They are transfixed in concerned inspection, the big eyes having focused on the awkward predator and the small brain translating the image as a threat. They leap into flight. The flush of one turkey is impressive; the flush of a large drove is pandemonium. Birds I had not seen materialize, and the six become twenty. All are airborne at the same time. Sometimes, one turkey will respond more slowly than the rest. Not this time. The flight is not graceful; yet in a very short time, a very large bird climbs through mature trees and is out of range. Incapable of any more productive action, I watch as the turkeys fan out in flight, each seeking its own path of escape. The surprise and the dense cover has resulted in effective dispersion of the drove. Scattered!

The turkeys gone, I sit down to collect myself and plan a strategy for the next episode. I check my watch. It is 3:30. I doubt if they will try to get back together before sunset; however, I will wait just in case. I construct a blind in the precise spot from which the drove flushed. I climb into the blind, allow my tired body to sink into the cool soil, and wait. Sunset comes quickly, and there is no indication that there is a wild turkey within five hundred miles. I awkwardly step out of the blind for the long walk back to the jeep. As I begin the descent, my mind drifts to the scattered young turkeys on the mountain, eager for the companionship the drove offers. Tomorrow should be the day!

Nell listens to her turkey hunter/husband's story and asks with a smile, "You wouldn't be going up there tomorrow, would you?" I smile back.

Despite the nine o'clock bedtime, I am numb as I grope through the room at 4:30 a.m. The anticipation of the scattered flock helps offset the fatigue, and I move to the kitchen with determination, if not grace.

A relatively short ride in the jeep, a long climb through the dark woods, and soon I am in the small blind. I ease myself into a comfortable position and wait for dawn.

Light comes, and I pull my body together against the now penetrating cold. I am tight with anticipation, because I am sure there will be turkeys calling on the mountain. The wait is short. The call is clear and unmistakable. It is the high-pitched whistle of the young turkey. The thrill of hearing the bird is tremendous. The challenge of making a good call is heightened by the knowledge that if you succeed the young bird will probably come running. The hours of practice with the call, and the successful

attempts in the past, give me confidence. I put the small diaphragm caller on my tongue and place it against the roof of my
mouth. I prepare my throat and mouth and then bring five quick
bursts of air from my lungs. The young turkey answers immedi-
ately, and I sense an urgency in its call. I prepare to respond, but
the call of another turkey, also below me but further to the right,
interrupts my preparation. I answer, and both turkeys scream
back with eagerness. The bird to the right calls again, and this
time he sounds perceptibly closer. I call back and try to interject a
sense of panic and urgency in the notes.

It is always such a great thrill to hear the bold, loud calls. The
second bird that answered is now coming steadily toward me, and
I shift my position in anticipation of his arrival. A dense clump of
laurel will prevent me from seeing the turkey until he is within
seventy yards of the blind. I wait, trying to control the now rapid
beating of my heart. I listen intently to the bird's call, and I pick
up the characteristic deep yelps with which the young gobbler
terminates his key-key call. At a range of what I guess to be a hundred yards, the bird lets out a series of loud whistles. I push the
gun forward until the blue rib and the tiny bead of silver are su-
perimposed on the tangle of laurel. I focus on the small bead, and
the laurel blurs into an impressionistic pattern of color. I hear the
distinctive two-footed gait as he comes. His approach is anything
but stealthy. He comes boldly, sounding like a quick-footed man
in the leaves. I move the safety off. I search frantically, as the
sound of his approach makes it impossible to believe he is not in
sight. The first visible indication of his presence is a flash of black
to the right of the spot upon which I have concentrated my attention. I adjust my body position slightly and look down the rib of
the shotgun. At fifty yards, the entire bird is visible, his body irri-
descent in the now higher sun. The turkey comes boldly toward
me. The long legs reach forward, and the bright eyes burn with
intensity. The tiny silver bead enters the bright picture, and I
place it under his head. The bird continues to stride toward me.
He is close enough. I feel the gun jar in my hands before there is
any distinct decision to shoot. After the instant blur, produced by
the heavy recoil, I refocus my eyes and see the broad, red-brown

tail fanned gracefully in the air. It is enough. I jerk myself from the confining blind and run, on cramped legs, to the dying turkey.

I am pleased to find the bird has been killed cleanly. Tiny points of bright red blood mark the large, blue head, providing vivid testimony to the effectiveness of the small shot. I inspect the wounds and then look at the entire bird. The myriad feathers shine in the bright sun. As always, I am particularly impressed by the size of the bird's eyes. I sit back and enjoy the warm satisfaction of the moment.

Turkeys can be killed by chance, but when they are killed consistently, it is not due to chance. I inspect the bird and relive the episode. I particularly cherish these calm moments. I celebrate my victory with a can of coke I carry in my pack for the occasion. I reflect on the accomplishment and I am unashamedly proud. I give humble thanks for being provided with the opportunity. I admire the wonderful bird. I enjoy my own company. Finally, I place the turkey's legs together, grasp them tightly in my right hand, swing him over my shoulder, pick up the shotgun and head down the slope.

I never have much trouble carrying a turkey out of the woods. I've killed a few large ones—one that weighed in excess of nineteen pounds—but the walk out has always been easy. The joy of victory is a great equalizer for fatigue. I move easily through the woods with the large bird on my shoulder. As I leave the woods, I transfer the turkey to my other shoulder and head down the logging road toward the jeep. I can't wait to take the bird back to Nell.

I hear the pick-up struggling up the road before I see it. It lurches into view, its metallic colors and harsh noises an obscene intrusion on the serenity. Three large men struggled to stay in their seats as the vehicle fights up the difficult slope. As I move to the side to let them pass, I pull the turkey up a little higher and try to appear nonchalant. The hunters don't pass. Three heavy men descend from the still moving car to see my bird. They wear new camouflage gear, and their guns are handsome. None has ever killed a turkey. They too are free to hunt turkeys for the first week of the season. The fatigue of one-and-a-half days of turkey hunting is visible in their faces. The men press close to examine my young gobbler. There is awe in their eyes as they inspect the beautiful bird. They ask the inevitable questions and then squeeze back into the pickup, their spirits and strength renewed. I watch their heads bob in animated conversation as the pickup surges up the road. I told them exactly where I had encountered the turkeys. They are confident, too confident. As I watch the awkward vehicle struggle, I smile to myself. Somehow, I know that my turkey will be the only one taken from the drove on this still-young fall day.

· 5 ·

The Spring

To many turkey hunters, the spring season is synonymous with turkey hunting. To other hunters, it adds another season to their sport. Regardless of the perspective, the behavior of wild turkeys in the spring allows the gobbler to be hunted without damaging the population.

For many of us not raised in the deep south, the idea of hunting in the spring season was, at first, strange. One morning with a hot gobbler and any doubts about the thrills of the spring will be quickly dismissed. For the beginner anticipating a spring hunt, it is important that he be aware that the techniques applicable to the fall must be altered for the spring.

The great advantage of the spring season is that the adult gobbler begins most mornings announcing his availability to any eligible hen. The gobble is used by the hunter to locate the bird. Even in good turkey range, turkeys are often hard to find in the fall. In good territory and with decent weather the spring hunter should be able to locate gobblers. The chances of locating birds will be enhanced by pre-season scouting. Extensive experience in an area will allow the intelligent hunter to locate specific areas that normally are used as roosting and breeding areas.

If you are planning a hunt to an area for the first time, I strongly urge you either to secure the services of a local guide or plan to spend two or three days finding birds.

Several tricks can be used to stimulate a reticent bird to gobble and hence give away his location. The owl call is a classic ploy. One can either learn to use his voice to imitate an owl or use one of the commercial calls on the market. I've had fine success with the little Olt plastic owl call. The call is particularly good before dawn. Gobblers will not always answer the call—in fact, one key lesson to learn about spring gobblers is that they are unpredictable—but in many instances they will.

THE ACOUSTICS OF THE GOBBLE

The same gobble that sounds as if it will shake the oaks at fifty feet will be barely audible if you are on the opposite side of a ridge from the bird on a moderately windy day. Under poor topographical and weather conditions, a gobble will not carry far. On many occasions my hunting partner and I have been shocked that the other did not hear a bird that was on the opposite side of a ridge. Also, the acoustics are altered significantly if the bird is in a tree or on the ground. Even the vegetation around the bird will alter the range at which the gobble can be heard. Do not overestimate the range at which a gobble will be heard. The call *does not* carry like the crowing of a rooster.

THE LISTENING POST

After a hunter has determined there is a gobbler or gobblers in an area, it is critical that he select a good spot from which to begin his hunt.

My hunting partners and I have come to call these locations listening posts. Invariably, a good listening post is situated so that the hunter can hear birds well and can move to the gobbler quickly and with the least chance of being detected.

The locations of two listening posts which have been very productive for us are marked on map number two. As the map shows, both these spots are relatively high and they offer the hunter easy access to several ridges that gobblers use for roosting. If you look at the map carefully, you will see that the locations allow the hunter to travel in several directions along relatively flat routes. This is particularly advantageous for two reasons. Steep travel is not only hard on the hunter but it is also noisy.

The listening post cannot be selected on the basis of geography alone. To be productive, it must be within a specific area that gobblers use in the spring. Finding a good listening post takes hard work. A topographical map will give clues to likely areas but one has to appraise a possible listening post in the field during the spring. There is no question that establishing good listening posts will improve one's success in the spring.

UNPREDICTABILITY

Before one is either discouraged by several frustrating hunts or conversely deceived by the success of his first hunt, it is important to understand that even for the best spring hunters there is an element of the unpredictable concerning mature gobblers. In many cases, the behavior of a gobbler will seem inexplicable. One could argue that no game is totally predictable; however, I would submit that the unpredictability characteristic of spring gobblers reaches another level. Adult gobblers will, occasionally, run to terrible calls. Other gobblers, under what seem to be perfect conditions, will refuse to come to what the hunter knows to be a highly effective call.

POOR ADVICE

I am convinced that it is the unpredictability of the birds in the spring that has resulted in so much poor advice being offered. Most advice you read for the fall is essentially valid; conversely, much of the advice you read concerning the spring is invalid. How many times have you heard or read, "call once, put up your gun and wait." Well, you will kill some turkeys following that suggestion but you will squander a lot of opportunities if you adhere to it without alteration. In many cases you should call more than once.

Reject the suggestion that you should always call from above the bird. It is true that there will be times when it is best to call from above, but at times it will be better to call from below. Many gobblers move down slopes to meet hens and they will do the same with you.

Forget the advice that one should never call at a bird on the roost. Making the right call at a bird on the roost will increase your chances of a kill significantly. Another rule, the adherence to which has provided many a hunter with silent mornings, is never to move from where you first call. At times, the best tactic is to move.

KEYS TO SPRING SUCCESS

The strategy of the spring caller is essentially simple: convince a mature gobbler that you are an eager hen. However, even after you have convinced the old boy, he may not come to you. Early in most spring hunting seasons gobblers are still accompanied by hens that have not yet begun to nest. The gobbler's bold calls at dawn receive an immediate response from various members of his harem. The hunter who has placed himself at a reasonable distance from the bird is often unaware of the fact that, as he makes his calls to the gobbler, three or four hens may be flying or walking right to the gobbling bird. The gobbler will often respond to every call the hunter makes while in the close company of his hens; however, his gobbles are sent to entice the reticent hen to do what all the others have just finished doing—coming to him. The gobbler just waits for that new, perhaps shy, hen to join the fun. The gobbler will strut, display, and occasionally approach the seemingly indifferent hens in his harem. It is true that a gobbler can be lured away from the hens, but this is rare. In this situation, the best tactic may be to wait patiently until the gobbler has enjoyed the company of his harem and then try to convince him that the new girl is worth a walk. The problem is for the hunter to determine whether or not the gobbler has a compliment of hens with him. Often the hens will make no loud calls. Also, even a gobbler without hens will not always come on a run to the first call he hears.

The time at which the hens go to stay with their nests is a key. Experienced spring hunters will recognize a short period of two or three days as being the *hot time* for their areas. Obviously, the date of kills is influenced by factors irrelevant to biology as well, such as weekends, and weather, but the *hot time* concept is important. Unusual weather patterns will upset the predictability of this situation, but if one has access to the dates of most kills over a five-year period a pattern may emerge. In one area in which I hunt, many of our kills have been on one calendar date. We believe this date corresponds to the time at which most of the hens have left the gobblers for continuous occupation of their nests. We have called spring birds up at other times, but we have particular confidence in this *hot time.*

When the hens go to the nest, a still eager gobbler finds he suddenly has lost his magic. He begins to get anxious about his virility. This is when the novice hunter squeaking out a rough series of yelps is suddenly presented with the startling presence of a twenty-pound gobbler running, with obvious purpose, directly at him. At such times more than one gobbler will often come to the call—occasionally, a gobbler will come an incredible distance to find the one hen still hungry for affection. In one case a friend and I had three beautiful gobblers come eagerly to our calls during one of these *hot times.* Two of these birds came long, long distances.

Obviously, many hunters do not enjoy the luxury of calculating, over a period of several years, when the *hot times* fall in a specific area. There is no answer to this problem. To be successful one must simply persevere.

SPECIFIC TECHNIQUES FOR WORKING A SPRING BIRD

Even early in the season the ever optimistic hunter hopes the bird he hears is, one, a mature gobbler and, two, isolated from hens. If the above are true, the best strategy is to get within one hundred to four hundred yards of the bird without being detected by him. The distance will be dependent upon terrain, cover, and the time of the day. Before light, in heavily wooded hills, the hunter may be able to get within one hundred yards of a bird with little risk of being detected. In contrast, late in the morning in flat bottom land the hunter may be detected if he trys to get closer than four hundred yards.

Once in position, at first light the hunter should make several tree calls or soft clucks. Usually these calls will result in exciting the gobbler, and he will begin to gobble or increase his gobbling. After his response to the call, particularly if it is a bold double gobble, the temptation is to call again. The best policy is to wait patiently, and in a position of readiness, for the bird to come to the ground. Often his desent to the ground will be audible; however, there are times when an easy glide and a soft landing will be made without a sound. The most dependable clue to his descent is the sound of his gobble. Even if he hops right to the base of the roosting tree, the variation in sound of the gobble should be apparent. It will be much more muffled when he is on the ground. At this juncture, it is time to make a quick series of hen yelps. I like a nice four-to-eight-note series of yelps that climbs the scale a bit. The timing and rhythm of this series is critical. If he gobbles back quickly, it is time to get ready. In some cases, you may need no more calls. If the bird hangs up, I will throw a quick cackle at him. In many situations, he will come very quickly; in others, his approach will be interminable. Once a bird without hens gobbled continuously from daylight on, and took three-and-a-half hours to come within range. During the period his gobbles, more than my calls, attracted another gobbler from such a distance that the second bird's first gobbles were barely audible.

You will be frustrated by situations for which there seems to be no explanation for a bird's decision not to come to you. An eager-sounding bird encountered late in the season when most of the hens are on their nests will simply walk away from you. Prepare for frustrations in the spring. There will be times when you can do nothing wrong, but I have found they are eventually balanced by strings of failures. One year I was trying a new call and called up six birds in a row. I had the answer! Unfortunately, I ran into a string after the six that had me wondering if I'd ever fool another.

THE YOUNG ONE-YEAR-OLD GOBBLER IN THE SPRING

The great percentage of birds that will come to your call will be mature turkeys of two years old or older. The one year bird with his three-to-five-inch beard will occasionally come to a call, but his response is usually very different from that of the mature gobbler. Often he will sneak in without a sound as you call to a gobbling bird that is some distance from you. Occasionally, he will yelp a few times and act as if he is simply interested in getting together with another turkey.

A young fall bird taking a look at the hunter.

A spring gobbler that came to within 20 steps of the caller.

Hunter in position from which he killed a fall bird. "Blind" consists of a patch of laurel in an old logging road. Young bird came to within 12 paces of the hunter.

Picture of a rough blind from which a fall bird was called and killed. The hunter is in the precise position as when he killed the bird. The contour blind concept was used so that the bird was not visible until it popped its head over the edge of the ridge at 20 paces from this crude blind.

Cold, +10° Fahrenheit, day in Decembe Heavy down coat, wool gloves, down hat, an wool pants are necessary if one must stay i blind for any length of time.

Two very large, 19-pound plus, gobblers killed in the spring. Bird on left had curved spurs 1¼″ long. Gun held is 10-gauge Beretta double.

Young bird of the year, killed in November, and the pre-war German drilling used to kill it. Gun was purchased from Paul Jaeger and Company, Jenkintown, Pennsylvania, a good source for European drillings and combination guns.

he big Ithaca magnum 10-gauge automatic
ıd a fall bird killed with it.

The rifle and the wild turkey. Young bird taken with 270 Winchester built by George Schielke on a pre-64 Model 70 Winchester action. Load used was the reduced one described in text.

The classic turkey rifle. A pre-1964 Model 70 Winchester in 22 Hornet caliber. Gun was made in 1949. It is probably the most efficient turkey rifle ever commercially manufactured.

10-gauge Beretta Magnum. My choice for the ideal turkey gun. The gun is chambered for 3½" shells and has 32" full choked barrels. It weighs 10 pounds 3 oz. with an Edwards recoil reducer in the stock.

Three fine turkey rifles. In the foreground a pre-64 Model 70 Winchester in 22 Hornet. Behind it a pre-Garcia Sako in 222 Remington. At the rear a pre-64 Winchester Model 70 in 243 Winchester caliber.

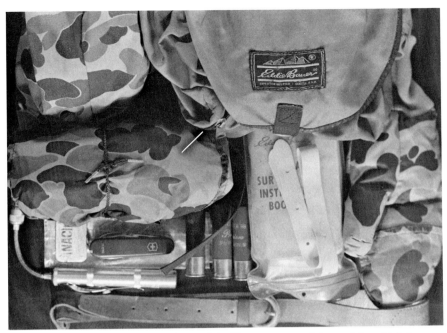

The day pack and its contents. The pack holds a one-pound down shirt which I carry in it during all fall and winter hunts. Other equipment pictured includes a one-pound survival kit which contains matches in waterproof container, a tube shelter, a whistle, first aid equipment, tea, sugar, soup, and honey, a compass, a mirror, a fire starter, a candle, and a collapsible cup. Other equipment includes a gun sling, a Swiss Army knife, a tourniquet, down gloves, down hat, 3 shotgun shells, an extra "Anacin" tin of diaphram calls, a flashlight that weighs 9½ oz. and a camouflage nylon ground shelter which measures 4 x 10′ with grommets at all the corners.

Entrance wound from copper-plated BB pellet.

Picture of the massive, 12¼ pounds loaded Ithaca 10-gauge magnum and a nice fall bird

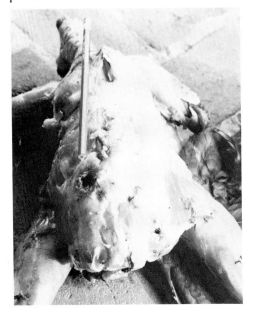

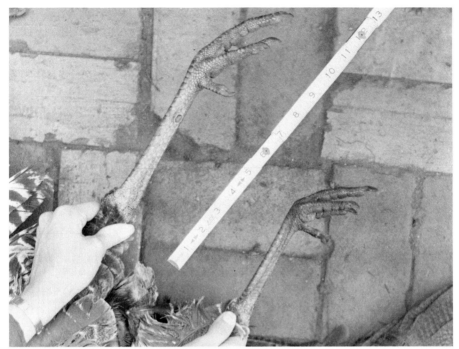

Variation in length and morphology of leg between sexes of immature, less-than-one-year-old birds killed in the fall. The gobbler leg on the left, with base of leg and human hands at bottom of photo, is much larger and heavier than the hen. Notice the tiny spur on the leg of the gobbler about 1½″ up the leg from the foot.

Effect of copper-plated BB pellet on head shot. Cranium of bird totally smashed by shot.

Tail of a mature turkey on right and immature, less than one year old, bird killed in the fall season. The even fan of the mature bird contrasts with the uneven fan of the young bird. As mentioned in the text this trait is visible at considerable distance when the bird is in flight. It represents one of the best ways to distinguish old birds from young in the field.

Comparison of size and shape of the head and neck of young birds of opposite sexes killed in November. Notice the more bulbous head of the gobbler, on the left, the reduced number of feathers on his neck, and the variation in the position of the eye relative to the depth of the face. Gobbler on left; Hen on right.

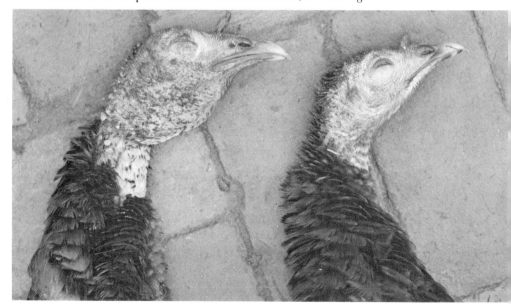

A picture that demonstrates all camouflage clothing is not equal in effectiveness! Notice how the light camouflage pattern on the right, worn by the taller hunter, does not blend with the background. Also, see how effectively the tiger stripe on the left breaks up the figure of the hunter despite the fact he is standing well in front of the cover.

This hunter's camouflage clothing, makeup and leaf-disguised hat have obviously paid off with a handsome turkey.

As this picture indicates, proper concealment combined with careful camouflage (plus silence and lack of movement) are key factors in successful turkey hunting.

The hunter's camouflage clothing and facial makeup blend the man into his background.

The author in his favored turkey-hunting clothes during a Spring hunt in Virginia.

Fall birds

Another picture of a Fall flock of Eastern wild turkey.

This is what it is all about—a Spring gobbler in full feather!

Going home.

If you are interested in killing a young gobbler, the best calls are the coarse gobbler yelp, and cluck. Such calls will also attract hens. In fact, be ready for hens to come to many of your calls. A subject not often discussed is the frequency with which mature hens will come to calls. Clucks and gobbles are, for obvious reasons, particularly conducive to attracting hens. Do not assume that the bird you hear walking to you is a gobbler!

TO MOVE OR NOT TO MOVE

Next to the problem of deciding when to call, perhaps the most difficult decision the spring hunter faces is when to move. The moving hunter is haunted by the idea of the bird coming directly to a place he just vacated. The stationary hunter agonizes over the bird's apparent movement away from him. For the solitary hunter, there is no answer to what to do in such situations. Unfortunately, no rule holds up. Occasionally, movement will result in a lost opportunity; however, movement sometimes offers the only hope.

If alone, I remain stationary unless the bird's movement suggest a purposeful orientation in a different direction. The move to head off a bird that moves away or parallel to your position should not be undertaken as a last resort. I have moved after a one-hour stalemate with a bird and made a call and had the bird come right to me. Why did the bird refuse essentially the same call from the other location? Unfortunately, the definitive answer rests with the bird that made the decision. I suspect it relates to his early experiences with the location of receptive hens. He calls from a place he expects them to come to, and when they fail to respond he moves to another courting area. When the hunter gets close to a courting zone, the bird is more likely to respond to his calls because they now come from a reasonable area. I have become a great believer in the fact that the hunter who learns which areas are courting zones will improve his success tremendously. The experienced hunter will be able to predict which zones are most likely to be used as mating areas, but occasionally the gobbler's selection of one area rather than others defies explanation. The knowledge of such areas may have done more to gain a hunter the reputation of being the world's best caller than any other thing.

Good gobbler roosting areas tend to be occupied on an annual basis in the spring. Killing a mature gobbler in one area certainly does not assure it will not be occupied the next year. By the same token, a productive roosting area is not always occupied.

I am confident that birds respond to pressure in the spring season. A bird that is exposed to similar calling on several days in a row will be unlikely to respond. However, hunting will not necessarily spook a gobbler. A bird that has ignored a man calling in a certain way four days in a row may run to a different call on the fifth day. The different call does not have to be a far superior one. I think it is often just the alteration in the call, not its inherent superiority, that may be most influential.

COMMON ERRORS OF THE SPRING HUNTER

1) Late entry into the woods has deprived many hunters of spring gobblers. For the man who enjoys a dawn walk to his hunting position, the spring gobbler season will provide a rude shock. You must be at your listening post at least one-half hour before *first light;* if you get in later than that you are in trouble.

2) Too much calling and too loud calling has scared many a spring bird. It is true some hens will send out loud calls during the spring, but for every loud call the hunter hears there are ten low-volume calls. The turkey expects soft calls most of the time. Many beginners try to answer a turkey every time he gobbles. Such a tactic will run off all but the hottest of birds. Under normal conditions the hunter should make low-volume calls and use them infrequently.

3) Trying to get too close to the bird is another common error. How many turkeys have been spooked by hunters who try to get close enough to see the bird? It is very hard to be silent in the predawn darkness of most turkey woods. Do not try to get too close to a gobbler.

4) Giving up the hunt after the first hour of light is another mistake. By giving up I mean hunting without confidence after prime time. Often the best time to catch a bird is after he has ser-

viced a hen and his desire is on the upswing again. It can happen at 9 a.m. or noon. If you have essentially packed it in at 8 a.m. and are carelessly wandering through the woods and calling, the chances of success are poor. Many birds are killed after 9 a.m. by determined hunters.

5) A common error of many hunters is the frequent use of special calls. If you have learned to make a nice series of yelps and have confidence in it, stick with it. I know you read all about the effectiveness of a cackle but unless your cackle is good it will do more harm than good.

6) Staying with a difficult bird day after day will prove very frustrating. If you enjoy the one-on-one challenge of such a match-up, that is fine; however, if you'd like to kill a gobbler, I suggest you send a friend after a bird that has frustrated you *for no obvious reason* over several days. There are some gobblers that simply will not come to a specific type of call. I am ready to admit there are some that are too tough for me. It took me some time to learn this lesson but it stuck.

7) Relying on an expert that has all the answers is a mistake. There are no never-fail calls, or callers. Anyone who hunts a lot and works at it will have a hot streak—and we all offer advice with more assurance during such times; but the success is temporary. The bird that will make a fool out of you is roosted out there right now.

8) Poor physical condition has ruined many spring hunts. The importance of physical condition varies with the environment in which you seek turkeys; however, in any situation it helps. Getting up at 3:30 a.m. will drain you even if you don't have to climb a steep ridge. Put a series of those 3:30 a.m. mornings together and you will separate the turkey hunters from the three-times-a-year boys. You will also eliminate most of those not in good condition.

9) Assuming that fooling a bird or two has given you *the answer* is another common fallacy. At times gobblers are easy to fool. The fact that they are has saved a lot of other turkeys. One friend had a hot gobbler run to him after making an outrageous noise on a gobbling call. When he came to see me with the bird he burned with the knowledge that he had found *the answer*. "He almost ran

me down, John. This is it, this is *the answer.* His eyes blazed with the zeal of the religious fanatic who has found the truth. For the rest of that spring and most of the next one, he scared gobblers from one side of the county to the other with the crazy call. Finally, succumbing to that special form of depression that is contracted only by frustrated spring turkey hunters, he sat across from me and with bowed head and dull eyes related the horror of his last twenty unproductive hunts. At the end of his tale of woe, I suggested that perhaps he should go back to his hen yelps and accept the fact that no gobbler will ever come quite as fast as the one deranged fellow that all but ravaged him the spring before. No, he didn't kill a twenty-pounder the next day, but he began to have some close calls. One morning about a week later I returned from an unsuccessful morning to see his car in our driveway. I didn't have to ask. My wife's smile, and his eyes, told me he was at peace with himself again.

Be careful about attributing too much to a success. There is no greater cure for the arrogant than a mature wild turkey gobbler—sex crazed or not.

A Successful Spring Hunt

My partner and I listened from the small saddle high above the long-deserted mountain farm. It was 4:25 a.m., and the only sound was our labored breathing as we tried to recover from the tough climb.

The first gobble was distant. The call was barely audible, but the sound erased our fatigue. Seconds later another bird announced his availability to the hens of Rockbridge County. This bird was also several ridges from our listening post. We waited hoping that the gobbler we had heard while scouting earlier in the week would still be on one of the two ridges that met at our saddle.

He waited until 4:40 to gobble. His location was, as usual, a surprise. Today, he was between the two ridges and four hundred yards below us. Jim and I discussed the situation in urgent whispers. The critical question of whether we should move closer to the bird dominated our quiet conversation. "I don't think he will come this far." "The slope is too steep, he will hear us if we try to get closer." "Do you think that is the same bird that was on the ridge?" "Let's stay." "OK."

Having made the decision to stay on the saddle, I felt for the small box that contained the diaphragm calls. In the darkness, I identified by feel the one I wanted and placed it in my mouth. It was cold. My first call was the soft tree yelp of a sleepy hen. There was no response from the obscure valley below us. We waited. After several moments of silence I glanced at the bright dial on my watch, 4:45. At 4:50, the bird gobbled again. It was a nice mature call. From the pitch of the call and its location, I was sure the bird was still on his roost. We waited.

Fifteen long minutes later, neither the bird nor I had called. During this time, the bird on the far ridge gobbled incessantly. In unashamed selfishness I hoped no other hunters would find him. The distant bird double-gobbled and I heard Jim move closer to me and I leaned toward the sound of his movement. He whispered, "That boy sounds hot, what do you think?" My answer was a supremely confident, "I don't know."

Our gobbler brought our attention back to the valley. He had waited long enough for the slow hen, and his gobble sounded impatient. He was still on the roost, but I sensed that this gobble had been directed to me and that he was eager. I prepared to call and felt the tension that prevails when you know a mature gobbler is waiting to hear you respond. My call sounded a bit high-pitched; it was followed by silence. My stomach began to feel empty. My confidence ebbed. It was now 5 o'clock and the trees and shrubs began to gain detail as more light came to the woods. We waited.

The next gobble jerked my head in the direction of the bird. The call was muffled. He was on the ground and he was closer! Jim's quick nod confirmed the assessment he read in my eyes. The gobbler was still two hundred yards away but now he was coming!

The cool morning began to penetrate my body and I trembled. I regretted my decision to leave the down shirt at home. I moved my body both to fight off the chill and relieve my cramped legs. I thought that some day I would think to sit in a position which would keep my legs from cramping. As I reflected on the thought, I smiled to myself, knowing that when I next sat down my only thoughts would be of the gobbler and I'd cramp my legs again.

At 5:15 I debated making another call. Ten minutes had passed and he might be expecting a flirtatious word from the hen. I decided to call as soon as he made his next gobble. I got impatient. I'd waited long enough for his cue. I pushed the little caller up against the roof of my mouth, took a breath, and tightened my stomach. He beat me to it. His gobble took the air from my chest and the call dropped from the roof of my mouth. He wasn't much more than a hundred yards away. I turned to Jim; his eyes were wide and his mouth partially open. Our eyes met and then we both turned to look out to the edge of the saddle. Below this ridge, somewhere, a gobbler was approaching. I heard Jim move slightly, and I shifted my weight as I pulled the big 10-gauge into position.

Five minutes passed. I strained to hear the sounds of his strut or his footsteps. I heard nothing. The woods were very quiet on this still, unusually cool spring morning. You can kill a lot of gobblers without hearing one gobble at less than a hundred yards distance. Many birds will make the last leg of the trip on the run, in strut, or moving at a slow walk. The majority do not gobble when they get close. Our bird was an exception. I recoiled at the gobble. It was so close the sound hit me with a physical force. I brought the 10-gauge up and looked down the barrel at the still lifeless edge of the saddle.

Jim and I both sensed the bird's presence before we heard him. I distinctly remember that the feeling he was there sent a surge of energy through my body and I was no longer cold. The sound of his footsteps was next. I strained to determine the precise direction to the sound. Soon he would pop up over the contour of the edge of the saddle. My hands tightened on the gun and I spoke to myself. "The challenge is to be cool and efficient." The footsteps stopped. The pressure increased. My eyes raced back and forth along the edge of the saddle. Suddenly, the footsteps began again and, an instant later, the great white head appeared.

Only a gobbler carries a head that size. It disappeared at the shot.

The next moment is blurred in my memory. I vaguely recall racing toward the bird I hoped I had killed. Jim's questions and comments bounced off my preoccupied mind. The bird was huge and very still. I was pleased he was still. I hate to have to watch a turkey die.

Victory! I thrust my fist in the air. It had been a while. In my excitement I bit the diaphragm call and bent it in half. I showed it to Jim and he said, "It would have made a great story if you had choked to death on that thing." We laughed louder than was necessary.

To say our discussion during the fifteen minutes was animated would be an understatement. A successful spring gobbler hunt is not conducive to relaxed conversations.

As the excitement cooled we paused to admire the bird. We have both seen a lot of turkeys, but for the next ten minutes we were engrossed in examination of the gobbler. We guessed his weight, fanned the great tail, measured the beard, felt the spurs, and stroked the soft, brilliant feathers. His spurs told us he was at least four years old, and I wondered as I always do what the four years had held for him. I reflected on the brutal winter storms he had survived and the predators, hunters included, he had eluded. I hoped he had enjoyed a good spring. The idea that several hens would raise his offspring in the months ahead was pleasing. Now that the intense thrill of the kill had begun to abate, I felt the warm satisfaction that comes with having done it well and knowing it.

A successful spring turkey hunt does not simply make a great day. It lasts. That afternoon I showed the bird to my family, the entire family. My two-year-old daughter and her seventy-year-old grandparents shared the excitement. Good friends came to see the gobbler that evening. I told and retold the story. Now, months after the bird was killed, I can still see its white head pop up above the ridge.

· 6 ·

The Well Prepared Turkey Hunter

One of the joys of turkey hunting is the anticipation implicit in preparation for the season. There are a variety of ways in which one should prepare. Physical preparation is essential. The dedicated hunter will also invest time and money in selecting equipment which will make him a more effective hunter.

PART ONE: THE PHYSICAL REALM

Occasionally, a hunter will harvest a turkey with only a modest investment of energy and effort. Most of the time the turkey hunter will earn the bird he kills. The physical strain imposed in earning a bird can be tremendous. It will vary not only with the specific hunt but also with the nature of the terrain in which an individual hunts. Usually, the area inhabited by turkeys is not the best for convenient human locomotion. The challenge may be topographical, with steep slopes and sharp ridges; in other situations, the challenge can be dense vegetation or poor footing. The problems of walking are compounded by the weight a turkey hunter typically carries. If you want to be impressed, weigh everything you carried and wore on your last hunt. I suspect it will weigh approximately thirty pounds.

The hunter can prepare himself for the strain imposed by walking long distances in difficult terrain by developing a regular program of physical conditioning. Many types of programs would be helpful, but a simple and efficient one is to run regularly. When I say run, I am not suggesting a slow jog around the block. To be in shape to face ridges and swamps you should regularly

] 95 [

run a good distance at a good pace. Obviously, you should check with your physician if you are not sure about your ability to take such stress. Two miles at a brisk pace is a reasonable goal. If your physician considers that too much for you, I believe the strain of most turkey hunting will be dangerous for you. You simply can't become a consistently successful hunter in both the fall and spring seasons and not be a strong walker. Find the consistently successful hunter in any part of the nation and, unless he is a brave elder statesman over sixty, I'll show you a strong walker. As a matter of fact, there are gentlemen in their sixties who will amaze you with their strength.

I try to run three times a week. I run just over two miles and I run it at what for me is a hard pace. Each person must develop his pace.

My only other conditioning involves scouting I do just prior to the season. I carry two cameras in my day pack and wear my hunting clothes and boots. The scouting is important and it is wonderful conditioning. No running on a flat surface will prepare you for hills. I'm aware that not many people are fortunate enough to be within fifteen minutes of good turkey habitat, but just before the season everyone should increase their physical exercise.

REST

The turkey hunter needs adequate sleep. If you are one of those people who believe that you need only two hours of sleep a day, I suggest you come down and hunt spring turkeys for a week and see how fit you feel at the end of the week. Spring turkey season is the greatest exercise in the world to convince man of his need for sleep. I am not speaking of two days of spring hunting; that is easy. I mean a solid week or two of rising at 2:30 or 3:30 a.m. Every man I've hunted with needed naps or an 8 p.m. bedtime to be reasonably efficient at the end of two hard weeks of a spring season. Again, I've read all the stories about turkey hunting in the morning and trout fishing in the afternoon. If you hunt turkeys the way they should be hunted in the spring, you will not have time, energy, or interest in trout.

DEVELOPING THE SENSES OF SIGHT AND HEARING

American Indian hunters were not born with fantastic senses of hearing and vision. They, as all other proficient hunters, developed the ability to interpret visual and auditory stimuli. You can learn to use your ears and eyes much more effectively. The ability to find game is not based exclusively on the acuity of vision or hearing. It is dependent on learning to search in the most likely locations and to interpret the keys that are there. You must learn not only what to look and listen for but also *how* to look and listen.

If you have ever watched an experienced eastern varmint hunter search a field for groundhogs, you will appreciate what I mean. He may have only average vision but he will locate ten animals to every one that the inexperienced person with 20-20 vision will find.

The experienced hunter learns where to concentrate his search. He learns what small parts of the animal look like. He also develops a capacity to identify what does not appear natural in a field. He registers changes in the field. If you have never hunted with someone who has developed such skill, your first exposure to this capability will be profoundly impressive.

While visual acuity is a great asset to the turkey hunter, there is probably no form of hunting where learning how to use one's hearing for the location of game is more important. Obviously, as with vision, some measure of physical capacity must exist for the skill to be developed; however, the key to performing well in this realm is learning to use your hearing. Some hunters can't identify the most common sounds in the woods. I have hunted with people who claimed to have killed turkeys who ignored the whistling call of the young turkey. It wasn't that they didn't hear the call, it was that they didn't know what it was. Others have jumped for cover at the calls of the pileated woodpecker or even the distant calls of a crow.

Many hunters have not developed the skill to distinguish between various species of animals as they walk on the ground. Anyone can be fooled once in a while, but anyone with just normal hearing can develop the skill to distinguish between the noises different creatures make in almost every instance.

The only way to develop such skills is to put yourself in a position where you will hear the sounds and to work at learning the differences.

PROTECTING ONE'S VISION AND HEARING

The wild turkey enjoys superb vision. What few writers stress is that human beings have fine vision as well. The gift of vision should be protected by the hunter. Turkey hunting imposes two serious threats to vision. The first is characteristic of all hunting with firearms. There are many ways in which a gun can propel gas, powder, or pieces of the shell or gun into a shooter's eyes. Barrel obstructions, faulty ammunition, and mechanical failures can all be culprits. Shooting glasses should be worn at all times by the responsible shooter. The margin of safety they provide is a great one and their cost is modest.

Shooting glasses also protect the turkey hunter from jamming branches into his eyes as he hunts. The chances of doing this are particularly good when one is rushing to get to a gobbler before dawn. People I have hunted with have had bad accidents doing just this. Protect your eyes. If you give a gun to your son, daughter or any young friend, put shooting glasses in the box. Fortunately, the quality of guns and ammunition is high and many people are simply lucky enough to avoid problems even when they do not take precautions. Don't bet on your luck—wear shooting glasses.

Unfortunately what we have said about the relative infrequency of accident to eyesight does not apply to hearing. Many individuals regularly engage in acts which destroy the acuteness of their hearing. Unlike vision, a moderate loss of hearing does not put one at a distinct disadvantage in most social circumstances. Oh, it may be embarrassing if the gun writer has to ask people to repeat sentences, but it is rare that great concern is exhibited over a modest loss of hearing. To the turkey hunter, even a modest loss is a serious disadvantage.

The second most difficult challenge in guiding is working with someone with poor hearing. (The most difficult challenge is the man who is in such poor physical condition he can't walk four hundred yards.) Many men who have worked on industrial jobs, used loud chain saws or power mowers, are avid pistol shooters or have listened to too many loud bands simply cannot hear turkeys call. Some people who might be described as having average hearing have lost their ability to hear at certain frequencies. At times it's hard to believe they can't hear birds call—but they can't.

If you are lucky enough to have good hearing, protect it! You don't have to live in a soundproof cave to do so. Many efficient and convenient devices exist that can protect hearing. The ear plugs that incorporate small valves are efficient and easily carried. I keep a pair in my car. At least once they allowed me to protect myself against noise levels that were certainly at the damaging level.

Don't shoot large bore guns often without some hearing protection. Don't shoot a pistol or high-velocity, large-bore rifle without muffs. I hunt doves, waterfowl and varmints with the small Lee Sonic valves in my ears. I can talk easily and hear anyone call me, but my ears enjoy a measure of protection. I don't use a chain saw or a mower without hearing protection. It is no less than tragic to see a sixty-year-old man in good health and condition who loves to hunt turkeys but can't hear them call. I know, I've hunted with one.

Even the young man can have very poor hearing. I'm sure the popular music of the 1960's and '70's has been a factor. Some who have trouble hearing birds tell me of rock concerts that produced days of ringing ears. Such a symptom, ringing over a period of several days, means irreversible hearing damage.

For many, the level of damage sustained by exposure to rock music or guns has no significant long-term effects; that is to say, they can perform their jobs and enjoy their hobbies without disadvantage. For any serious turkey hunter, the effects are catastrophic.

PART TWO: EQUIPMENT NEEDS

CLOTHING

Many of my avid turkey hunting friends will smile at the concept that special attention needs to be made to clothing. As one recently said, "John, you're the only guy I know who wears those gloves and camouflage pants and jacket and still kills a few turkeys." The sentence holds an important lesson; clothing does not make the turkey hunter. The best clothes are no substitute for experience and the skill that should accompany experience. All other things being equal, however, the man who pays attention to what constitutes good clothing is at a distinct advantage.

FOOTWEAR

The one area that is critical to any hunter is the quality of his footwear. As the case with all clothes, appropriate footwear is area-specific. What is best in the rugged mountains of eastern West Virginia is not best in the warm, wet swamp of Louisiana.

For hard rocky mountains, the Vibram sole is indispensable. If those limestone outcrops are wet, travel is tough in Vibrams and impossible in anything else. I like uninsulated leather boots with firm steel counters and a counterset heel. My last pair of Gokey boots, the fourth pair I have received great service from over the last two decades, cost a bit more than a Model-70 Winchester I bought in 1957. That is a hell of an investment but if one hunts the ridges of the Appalachians, from New York to Georgia, he will only be as good as his boots. I would seriously rather hunt with a single-shot shotgun and a superb pair of boots with Vibram soles than with a Purdey and a pair of tennis shoes. In the wrong boots, you will cripple your feet in two hours in our hills.

Other areas and environments are less demanding. In many situations, an inferior pair of boots will simply impose a bit of discomfort that can be endured, but if you plan to hunt in a tough area I submit that you had better invest in superb boots.

Another major mistake made by turkey hunters is that they select boots designed to provide maximum comfort under intense cold. Some turkey hunters will face intense cold, but it is rare that they need the insulation demanded by the immobile deer or duck hunter. Most turkey hunters are on the move at least some of the time. When selecting boots, don't forget the spring season! Temperatures will often be high in the spring. You will still need the Vibram soles, but heavy insulation will make feet perspire and cause a variety of discomforts.

I am a firm believer in wool socks for all but the warmest times of the year. Wool holds the moisture away from your body and has the magical quality of maintaining heat even when wet. In the spring, I wear thick fleecy cotton socks.

Obviously, the clothes appropriate for fall and winter hunters will be distinctly different from those appropriate to the spring.

THE FALL AND WINTER

I am a wool addict. As mentioned above, it is warm while wet and it keeps perspiration away from your body. In addition, it is quiet. I have had men in a blind with me who sounded as if they were sitting on a bag of pretzels because the synthetic materials in their clothes were so noisy. Nylon and canvas are all right in some situations, but they both make a lot of noise. Before you buy that coat or pair of pants, grab a handful of the material or run a fingernail over it. If the sounds produced are loud, it will put you at a disadvantage in the turkey woods.

I like light wool pants and shirts for the fall. The best pants I have found are made by the Filson Company in Oregon. They are durable, light, woven dark-green foresters' pants. After a week's hunt in them they still look and feel good. They are warm but not too warm. I like the light-weight wool shirts in dark green made by Pendleton. On a relatively cool day, with a high in the 40's or 50's, I will wear the wool pants, a light wool undershirt and the light wool shirt. A down shirt is carried in my pack. The down shirt stays in my pack unless I have the good fortune to scatter a flock. In such a situation, I put the down shirt on under the wool shirt and it keeps me comfortable. If the stay is for over a couple of hours, I will get cool but it will not be unendurable.

To wear or carry more on a regular hunting day would have me sweating and miserable in no time. Walking and burning calories in turkey country will heat you up in a hurry.

The hat I wear is a light cotton army fatigue cap. As long as I am moving, it is rare that it is not warm enough. I also wear light leather shooting gloves, more for purposes of hand camouflage and protection against brush than for warmth.

In my pack, I always carry a camouflaged down-filled hat and a pair of down gloves. If I do scatter turkeys and build a blind, these two items of apparel go on when the down shirt does. It is amazing the effect that the warm down hat and gloves can have on your total body comfort. For a time I thought the advantage was psychological, but a physiologist friend told me that the hat and gloves will help preserve a great deal of body heat.

During the fall and winter, I also keep a large day pack filled with the gear I use the morning after I have scattered a flock. In such a situation, I will be in my blind before dawn and, particularly if the group of birds scattered happens to be a flock of gobblers, there is no telling how long I will wait in the blind. Under such circumstances, the clothes I wear on a searching hunt are totally inadequate. When I go into the woods I wear what I normally hunt with, except for my boots, which are of insulated leather. I will wear one pair of silk and two pair of wool socks. My pack will carry a heavy down-filled parka and a pair of down-filled overalls. The overalls have zippers on the legs and can be pulled over my boots. Both garments are designed to provide comfort at well below zero temperatures. When one begins his wait in the pre-dawn darkness of an Appalachian ridge, they will be none too warm. You must *carry* the heavy gear into the woods. If you wear it, you will be saturated with sweat as you sit down in your blind. And while wool maintains heat when wet, its insulating qualities are reduced. I have watched many hunters suffer as they shivered in the blind because of a combination of walking in with too many clothes and wearing cotton next to their skin. They have laughed at me when I left the vehicle with a light wool shirt and wool pants in the 20-degree pre-dawn darkness. Sure I am cold for the first two hundred yards, but it doesn't take long for me to be reasonably comfortable and later I will be dry and warm.

My rain gear consists of a heavy wool sweater. I refuse to allow my wife to have it laundered. It still has the natural lanolin in it and repells water, but it lets my body breath. I can't stand the clammy feel of rubber or truly waterproof nylon. They are fine in a duck blind or on a boat but if you are walking—no thank you. I don't even like to carry them to use on a stand. They are too noisy and shiny. A leaf camouflage pattern is no good if it is on shiny nylon. I like my heavy sweater. I get a bit warm with it on but on a cold dreary day it is a fair trade off.

I take only the sweater when it is rainy or promises to rain or snow. If I get caught in an unexpected rain, I get wet and hunt; my wool keeps me warm. If you are dressed in cotton you will be miserable in a light rain.

One extra item I carry with me in my pack is a pair of socks. On an all-day hunt, I change socks at lunch. This step provides a lift for me, particularly if it is warm.

THE SPRING

In most areas late March, April and early May are delightful times of the year. Cold weather is unusual, although in the northern states and even as far south as some of the southern Appalachian states you can get frost and an unusual cold day or two in April. For a typical warm spring day, light cotton clothes are fine.

I have found that army cotton combat clothes with tiger-stripe camouflage are excellent. I have used those I received during my Army tour in the 1960s. It is supplemented by equipment purchased from surplus outlets. I like the olive-drab Army teeshirts of soft cotton. My M-65 fatigue jacket has served me well, as have the tiger-striped shirts and pants. In my opinion, they are of better quality—that is the honest Army issue material, not the copies—than most of those I have seen that are commercially produced.

If you can find a pair of Vietnam boots with the nylon tops and Vibram-type sole, you will have a superb warm-weather turkey boot. The cotton socks, handkerchiefs, and tiger-stripe hats that so many of us took for granted in the Army are really first rate. Don't just buy the first cheap camouflage pattern shirt or pants you see. Many are of inferior quality. The colors are poor, the dyes run, and the garments are not durable. There are high quality camouflage clothes made commercially, but you better make sure you have acquired one of the quality types. Avoid very light patterns of camouflage. For most areas, a *non-fading* tiger stripe cannot be improved upon.

ACCESSORIES FOR THE TURKEY HUNTER

Many superb turkey hunters have ventured into the woods with an inventory of accessory equipment that consists of a pocket knife. However, there are other items that the well equipped turkey hunter should carry. They will be worth the space and weight. Weight is the critical factor. Turkey hunters usually must cover a considerable amount of ground and they can ill-afford unnecessary weight.

The accompanying photograph shows the equipment I carry on all my turkey hunts. Hunting over a series of years has resulted in each piece of equipment earning its place. Included in my day pack are the following:

1) A survival kit. I have carried the kit in the picture for four years. I've never needed it and my only use of it has consisted of familiarizing myself with its contents. This particular kit was marketed by Eddie Bauer. It weighs one pound.

I firmly believe no turkey hunter should venture out alone without such a kit. The importance of the kit is not predicated on the isolation of the area in which you hunt. A broken leg five hundred yards from an interstate puts your life in jeopardy if you must face much time without cover or fire. The plastic tarp, matches, fire-starting materials, and signal mirror in the survival kit could save your life.

2) A down shirt. I carry this one-pound garment in my small day-pack at all times, regardless of weather. There are several makers of such items. Unlike other parts of my survival pack, the shirt is used in non-emergency situations. It can be considered relevant to survival because it is such a major conserver of warmth. The shirt is packed in a small plastic garbage bag. The bag provides added protection against the garment getting wet and doubles as a game bag.

3) A sling for my gun. I have a detachable sling that is carried in one of the pockets of my pack. If the gun does not have a swivel, the loop slings that are available from a number of makers are perfectly adequate. The only disadvantage with the loop sling

is that when attached to the gun the front loop will often block out the front sight.

4) Two extra diaphragm turkey calls. These are always carried in a small "Anacin" tin in my pack. Someday you will misplace your regular call or lose it on the floor of the car.

5) First aid items. I have found most first aid kits inadequate. I carry two tourniquets of adequate size and a half dozen bandaids. In packaged first aid kits, the bandaids are rapidly used up while nothing else is ever used. The tourniquets are elastic ones that will allow you to deal with a serious hemorrhaging injury, and they also can be used to construct a splint.

6) A down hat, down socks and a pair of down gloves. The down gloves and socks weigh next to nothing but could save you from frostbite. I make use of these items in more than survival situations; however, they are always in the pack regardless of how unseasonably warm an October or November day might be.

7) A Silica Explorer's compass wrapped in a green army surplus handkerchief. The compass, and of equal importance the ability to use it, are valuable to the turkey hunter for obvious reasons. One comment about the survival implications is that you should not assume that familiarity of a given hunting area obviates the need for a compass. Until a low dense fog has suddenly enveloped you on a familiar piece of hunting range, it is impossible to really appreciate a compass.

Even in non survival situations a turkey hunter will reap the benefits of a compass. As an example, in some instances you will want to follow a turkey or turkeys that you have flushed. If, as happened to me on one occasion, the turkeys fly over a series of small ridges, an azimuth reading from your compass may be the only way to follow the birds.

In addition, a compass will allow the hunter to map the area he hunts. The primary tool used in the constuction of the maps I made for this book was a compass. Such a map not only is a help to a specific hunter but is also invaluable when the hunter is introducing his area to friends unfamiliar with it.

8) A compact and durable flashlight. The tiny flashlights that operate on two AA batteries are perfect for the turkey hunter.

One is pictured in the accompanying photo. It was designed for operations in the cockpit of an aircraft. It is durable, lightweight, and has a functional lanyard.

9) Three shotgun shells. These are not part of my normal complement of shells for a day's hunting.

10) An extra key for the ignition of my car. I carry the extra key for my car taped in my wallet. Once while hunting alone in an isolated section of a neighboring state, I lost the keys I carried in my pocket. I was so proud of the fact I had the extra key taped in my wallet, it made me overlook how careless I had been to lose my original key. I've often reflected on just how difficult it would have been without that key. At the time I was a bachelor, eight hours from my home, in an area in which I knew no one.

EQUIPMENT THAT IS NOT NEEDED:

1) A big belt knife. The large knife indicates the individual carrying it has made the decision to carry two pounds that have no function.

2) A side-arm of any caliber is worthless weight to the turkey hunter armed with a rifle or shotgun. It is surprising how many hunters, especially young ones, I encounter walking through the woods with large side-arms. The side-arm not only adds weight, it also imposes a danger. Even when handled by the competent, a side-arm is dangerous. The last comment is obviously not made by an anti-gun freak. It is made by one who carried a side-arm on a daily basis for two years in the Amazon basin and who served as a military police captain for two years. I know a little bit about the number of accidents that accrue from hand gun use. Also, unless you have the discipline to wear hearing protection *at all times,* a hand gun will damage the hearing that is so critical to your success as a turkey hunter.

3) A large flashlight. This piece of equipment indicates the bearer has little concern for the stress he places on his body. It also suggests the hunter may not be above looking in the tops of trees for roosting birds. The handy, compact flash is perfect for finding your way through the woods and absolutely inadequate to the task of locating birds in the top of a hundred-foot oak.

4) A turkey sling. I've carried my share of birds from the field and I've felt no loss in not having a turkey sling. The main compartment of my day pack provides a suitable place for all but the largest of turkeys. The accompanying pictures show me with birds effectively accommodated in that pack. If I kill a large gobbler that will not fit in the pack, I sling my gun and carry the bird by its feet. The task is not difficult. I've had some long walks over some rough country with some big birds but the task has never been impossible. Excellent companies that produce fine calls and equipment that I use also produce turkey straps. I believe the straps are unnecessary.

5) A camera. As the photographs indicate I take a lot of pictures of my turkey hunting. When guiding hunters I will frequently carry a camera; however, when I am hunting the camera is just too much weight for me. I know you can get a compact camera, but it is not essential for hunting and when my lungs scream as I try to go over one more tough ridge I want to know that all the weight I carry is necessary.

· 7 ·

Guns and Loads
for Turkey Hunting

PART ONE: THE SHOTGUN

The wild turkey is, quite simply, more difficult to kill than any other North American game bird. A primary factor contributing to the turkey's relative invulnerability is his great size. In most areas, a ten-pound goose is considered large; in contrast, even in their first fall season few gobblers will weigh as little as ten pounds. Most mature spring gobblers weigh between fifteen and twenty pounds. My average for mature spring gobblers has been eighteen pounds three ounces. I know you have read about twenty-eight pound birds, but the largest I have ever seen weighed exactly twenty-one pounds. An eighteen-pound bird is constructed with very heavy bones and thick muscle. The very bulk of the creature makes him a formidable challenge for shotgun pellets.

There is nothing to suggest that the turkey's tenacity for life is not comparable to his great size; on the contrary, pound for pound only the pheasant, of all other game birds, compares to the turkey.

A primary reason turkeys are unlikely to be killed cleanly when hit in the body is that they are so often shot while standing on the ground. In such a posture, the heavy wings protect the vital organs of the visera. Also, the vulnerable under-belly area, so often exposed by waterfowl when the birds fly over the hunter, is rarely presented.

] 109 [

THE INVULNERABILITY MYTH

An exaggeration of the toughness and tenacity of the turkey has resulted in the popular acceptance of a myth of invulnerability. Frequently, the aspiring turkey hunter will be told, "the only place a turkey is vulnerable is his head. Shooting at a turkey's body with a shotgun is foolish, the pellets can't penetrate the body." The last statement is ridiculous. Large shot, size 3's, 2's, and BB's, propelled at normal velocity, 1150 to 1300 feet per second (fps), will devastate a turkey at reasonable range. A BB pellet from a typical magnum load strikes a turkey at forty yards with a force of approximately fifteen foot pounds. Table 2 indicates that at this range the pellet penetrates an average of twenty-five double ply cardboard sheets ⅛-inch thick. I can assure you from the anatomical studies I have conducted that it will easily penetrate the body cavity of the largest turkey from any angle. Let me stress that I am not making a case for the effectiveness of *size 4 or smaller shot* on the body of the turkey but rather size 3's, 2's, and BB's.

I will not provide you with the details of the autopsies I have conducted; however, I have collected data on every bird I have killed and most that have been killed by the many hunters I have guided. Suffice it to say, BB shot will smash the vertebrae column, crush any of the bones that make up the cranium, and shatter the largest of the bone of the legs, the tibiotarsus.

To provide a specific example of the penetration of BB shot, a shot at a bird flying directly away at an estimated thirty-five yards resulted in a clean kill. Pellets were found in the craw of the bird, attesting to total penetration of his body.

Since adopting the BB, 10-gauge load for both myself and hunters I have guided, it has been used to kill eight turkeys. Not a single bird has been lost. The average range has been a long forty-nine yards. Of the eight birds killed, only one was capable of coordinated movement after the shot. (The long average range is a function of the fact that this is the load I use in the left barrel of my 10-gauge double, hence it is selected for long-range opportunities.)

For anyone familiar with the tenacity of turkeys, a record that shows a recovery of eight for eight at an average range of forty-nine yards, with the closest shot at thirty-five and the longest at seventy-five, constitutes a great tribute to the effect of the load.

I believe in large shot in both barrels. My right barrel load in the 10-gauge uses 2½ *ounces* of number three shot. There are 273 of the number three shot in this load. Propelled by 38.0 grains of blue-dot powder, the load generates tremendous energy. The heavy shot charge reduces velocity but it chronographs at a very respectable 1129 fps—just about the speed of the fine factory 2¼-ounce loads that have been on the market since 1977. Incredibly, there are almost the same number of the big number three shot in this load—273—as there are number six shot in the standard 1¼-ounce 12-gauge load, 279. At fifty-five yards, each number three shot will penetrate an average of eight sheets of two-ply cardboard sheets ⅛ inch thick, while the number six shot will penetrate an average of only four. To gain a wide pattern and reduce the pressures, I load the 2½ ounces of number three shot without a collar or buffer filling. This produces even 66 percent patterns from my full choke barrel at forty yards.

This number three load is my choice for shots to a full fifty yards. At fifty yards, it produces lethal patterns. At this range, my 2⅛-ounce BB handload load is still giving 70 percent patterns which are a bit too tight.

Eight turkeys have been hit with my number three load. The average range has been a modest twenty-eight yards. The longest shot was sixty-five yards, the shortest ten. Of the eight birds hit, only one was lost. This shot was taken at forty yards in thick brush. Of the seven birds killed, only one was capable of coordinated movement after the shot—this was the bird shot at a range of sixty-five yards. All seven birds were easily recovered. This is an excellent load for 90 percent of the opportunities the turkey hunter will encounter. The pattern is not too tight, and the individual shot has tremendous energy. Indicative of the energy of the pellets is the fact that at ranges up to fifty-five yards the shot will break the largest bones in the turkey's body. It will not smash the skeleton as BBs will, but it will break large bones. By comparison, at the fifty-five-yard range, number four shot will not break heavy bones. At the normal ranges to which birds are called, the number three's will also completely penetrate the head and neck. The last bird I killed with this load was a 13-pound young gobbler walking directly toward me at a range of approximately thirty yards. The number three load put twelve pellets in the head and neck. These pellets exited from the turkey. Approximately fifteen pellets struck the body. The right tibiotarsus was broken in two places, and several pellets cut fibers from the bird's three-inch beard, penetrated the craw, and exited after going through the upper part of the body. Several pellets that penetrated the chest area were found deep in the viscera. This is a superb load.

THE IMPLICATIONS OF BRUSH

An extremely significant, but rarely discussed, factor reducing the effectiveness of shotgun on turkeys is brush deflection of pellets. The hardwood forests, swamps, and scrubby plateaus that comprise good turkey habitat invariably present brush that is capable of deflecting, impeding, and stopping shot. Often the shot that appears to be open will be screened with light vegetation. If you appreciate and respect the fact that brush can deflect a rifle bullet, test what it does to the much lighter shotgun pellet! A lack of understanding of the effect brush can have on shotgun pellets, and the patterns they comprise, is a major factor contributing to the non-fatal wounding of turkeys.

Table One presents data relevant to the performance of shotgun loads through brush. These data not only indicate the significant reduction in the effectiveness of *all loads* but also demonstrate the implications of pellet size.

The dense cover that causes problems of brush deflection also provides an environment in which it is easy to lose a bird. Invariably, there are numerous hiding places that even a mortally wounded bird can seek without moving far from the spot where it fell. Before the significance of this point is lost, the hunter should reflect on the ease with which he could recover his wounded pheasants or geese if the birds invariably fell into a dense hardwood forest! In addition, the probability of losing a bird is compounded by the fact that very few turkey hunters have a

TABLE ONE

BRUSH DEFLECTION DATA

(40 yard range 2 screens light brush, 5 and 10 yards in front of target)

10 Gauge 3½″ magnum
Ithaca Automatic no. 0000 4229
2⅜ oz. BB shot (116 pellets) 32″ full choke
Average velocity chronographed: 1299 feet per second

12 gauge 3″ magnum
Browning Superposed no. 9431758
1⅝ oz. no. 6 shot (366 pellets) 30″ full choke
Velocity published as 1315 feet per second

	10 Gauge	12 gauge
Without Brush / 5 shots	shot 1 — 106 pellets in 30″ circle 2 — 105 3 — 108 4 — 103 5 — 97 Average 104 9.5 percent variation **90% on target**	shot 1 — 264 pellets in 30″ circle 2 — 249 3 — 231 4 — 227 5 — 220 average 238 12.0 percent variation **65% on target**
With Brush / 3 shots	shot 1 — 65 pellets in 30″ circle 2 — 70 3 — 89 Average 75 20.5 percent variation **65% on target**	shot 1 — 120 pellets in 30″ circle 2 — 118 3 — 102 average 113 1.9 percent variation **31% on target**
Brush Influence	clear shot 104 pellets → brush shot 75 pellets brush influence - 28 percent loss of pattern density	clear shot 238 pellets → brush shot 113 pellets brush influence - 53 percent loss of pattern density

retrieving dog as a companion. In fact, in many states laws prohibit the use of a dog while turkey hunting.

All of the above factors combine to produce a situation conducive to the frequent loss of crippled birds. While the crippling of any game bird is tragic, the loss of the majestic wild turkey is particularly disturbing.

The only way in which the losses of the birds can be reduced is to invest the time in a careful analysis of what in fact does constitute the most efficient shotgun and load.

THE SMALL SHOT FALLACY

Pick up a book or article on turkey hunting and with rare exception it will suggest that the hunter use small shot; frequently, number six is recommended. My research indicates that such advice is probably responsible for the crippling of many turkeys.

The small shot advocates present the following argument: Since small shot will effectively penetrate the vulnerable head and neck of a turkey at reasonable range, the hunter should aim only at the head and refrain from shooting at ranges over forty yards. The claim is that such a strategy is an exercise in conservation since large shot advocates might shoot at birds over forty yards and wound them.

One of the major problems with the small shot philosophy is that few hunters are capable of estimating, with precision, a distance of forty yards. A turkey at fifty yards, particularly if the bird is in the air, looks close. There is no question that many birds perceived to be at a range of forty yards are in fact shot at ranges of fifty and more. Also, how many hunters will in fact resist a shot at a turkey at fifty yards? Remember, this is not a goose pit where another flock may come by within range in twenty minutes. The turkey you refuse to shoot at may be the last chance you have this year. It is fine to argue that turkey hunters should not take a shot over forty yards, but I don't believe the advice will be followed. This is not to suggest that turkey hunters cannot be persuaded to adopt a realistic maximum range; however, the forty-yard limit imposed by small shot advocates is not enough. In many cases, the bird at fifty yards will be standing on the ground, so the valid argument articulated by the waterfowl hunters concerning the inability of all but experts to hit at over forty yards does not apply. The fact that you may have killed a turkey, or turkeys, at over forty yards with number six shot does not obviate the fallacy of the small-shot philosophy. I too have killed turkeys at over forty yards with sixes. However, when I used sixes I also lost turkeys shot at what I judged to be forty yards. If you take chances at what you estimate is forty yards with sixes and shoot at ten turkeys, you will wound at least one—period.

Another problem is that a turkey within forty yards of the blind will not always be so obliging to present his head and neck to the hunter. As experienced hunters know, occasionally turkeys will sneak close to the blind only to flush upon perceiving that something is amiss. In these instances, the hunter will frequently be presented with a thirty-yard shot at a turkey flying directly away from him. Again, I ask that we be realistic about the likelihood that the hunter will resist such an opportunity. If you have worked the bird for three mornings and on this day it has taken two hours to call him, are you going to pass up a shot at thirty yards? It's true there is a good chance the sixes will kill him; however in many cases the bird will be mortally wounded but will sail eight hundred yards to die. In this situation, larger shot, such as that in the loads discussed above, will produce a bird that will not maintain flight after being hit.

A particularly critical fact is that even when the head and neck are exposed at forty yards, light brush can deflect and disrupt the shot pattern so that a non-lethal wound will be inflicted. By light brush I mean just that. Frequently, a shot will appear to be open and yet the shot charge will be interrupted by brush and small saplings at from six to twenty, *yes* twenty, places along the short forty-yard distance. The next time you kill a bird on the ground, check the number of times the shot pattern cut through brush, twigs, and saplings on the way to the bird. I've done it and I know you will be impressed. The point is that heavy shot penetrates brush much more effectively than does light shot. Again, look at Table One. I believe these data make the point more effectively than lengthy discussion. All experienced turkey hunters who began hunting with small shot have been shocked by the loss of a bird shot at some thirty-five yards from the blind, in what appeared to be a relatively open area. The spot the turkey occupied at the time of the shot will provide evidence of a hit in the form of one to a half-dozen light breast and lower neck feathers. I am convinced brush is the culprit.

Another problem our small-shot hunter faces is what to do when a bird flushes to present a crossing shot? If you tell me that he will hold for the head and neck, I will suggest that most shooters, good ones included, will shoot at the total bulk of the turkey. A shotgun is swung through a total target, not part of it. Hence most hits will be in the body. With number six shot, the turkey had better be within forty yards if you expect to knock him down from the air. If it is over that range, the shot does not maintain the necessary energy to break heavy bones. I have hit turkeys with a first barrel of sixes, only to have them fall after a second hit with number two's. In these cases, I have not assumed the sixes hit, but rather found them in the bird. Sixes will simply not break up the physical structure of the bird at ranges over thirty-five yards.

When I suggest large shot is the best answer, again I stress *large* shot, three's, two's and BB's. As indicated above, my experience indicates that even number four shot is too light to be a good choice on this huge bird.

A critical fact concerning three's, two's and BB's is that there is nothing inherently ineffectual about large shot aimed at the head and neck! One of the great fallacies implicit in the small-shot philosophy is the concept that it is difficult or impossible to shoot a turkey in the head or neck with large shot. The idea is ridiculous.

Out to forty-five yards, three's, two's and BB's provide adequate pattern density to assure hits in the head and neck. You won't get as many hits as with six's but you don't *need* as many. In fact, you will be surprised how many hits will be produced. The last bird I killed with a 12-gauge gun was taken with a 1½-ounce load of two's in a standard length, 2¾-inch twelve. The bird came, as many will, to within twenty yards of me. I put nine of the big number two shot in the bird's head and neck. Was I at a disadvantage with my tight load of two's? The instantly killed turkey suggests that I was not. Granted, if I had used sixes I would have killed the bird, *but* what if the bird had flushed at the last moment and offered a departing turkey target? If I had done my part, the two's would have killed the bird neatly. If I had done my part with the six's, there is a good chance I would have lost the bird. Would I have passed the bird up with six's? I doubt it.

Even with the large BB's, I have also found that turkey heads and necks are not impossible to hit. The head and neck are not *that* small. On one mature gobbler I measured carefully, the area comprised a full 12¼-inch area. A good dense pattern of BB's will put at least two pellets in this target at forty yards. I've tested this question and it is simply a fact. It is not impossible to hit the head of a turkey and neck of a turkey with large shot! In the 10-gauge, I have 116 pellets in my 2⅛-ounce BB load. In my 12-gauge load, I have between 111 and 178 number two pellets, depending upon whether I am using a 2¾-inch or 3-inch gun. With this pellet count, head and neck hits to forty yards should be, and for me have been, a sure thing.

To address the question of the applicability of large shot to the head and neck, let us look at the problem mathematically. Table Two indicates that my 2⅛-ounce buffered 10-gauge load provides 90 percent patterns in an unaltered Ithaca automatic. To calculate the density of the 90 percent BB load at forty yards on the assumption that the distribution within the 30-inch circle was even would be erroneous. The average number of pellets within a twenty-inch circle, within the thirty-inch circle, for the 10-gauge loads documented in Table Two was seventy-two. There are approximately 314 square inches within the 20-inch circle, and an average hit of one per every 4.4 square inches is achieved. With a head and neck size of 12.5 inches we can expect, and in fact shots at mock up turkey heads at the range will give you, an average of three pellet hits per head. Needless to say, this is adequate. At all ranges under forty yards the density of the pattern, and the ease with which the head is hit, increase. If the bird hangs up at between forty and fifty-five yards I aim where the neck enters the body and the three's, two's or BB's will produce a dead bird. With the BB load in the 10-gauge, *but not the number two load in the twelve,*

TABLE TWO
LARGE SHOT EFFICIENCY
(same guns and loads as in Table One)

RANGE	Mean number of pellets in 30 inch circle		Mean percentage of pellets in 30 inch circle		Percentage loss from 40-yard efficiency		Number of pellets in vital areas of 12¾ lb. turkey		Energy per pellet in foot pounds		Foot pounds of energy delivered to 12¾ lb. turkey		Average number of ⅛ inch 2 ply cardboard sheets penetrated	
	10 gauge	12 gauge	10 gauge	12 gauge	10 gauge	12 gauge	10 gauge	12 gauge	10 gauge	12 gauge	10 gauge	12 gauge	10 gauge	12 gauge
40 Yards 5 shots	104	238	90%	65%			9	21	15	2.5	135	53	25	6
50 Yards 3 shots	81	157	70%	43%	23%	23%	7	14	13	2.0	105	28	20	5
60 Yards 3 shots	59	96	51%	26%	31%	60%	5	8	11	1.5	55	12	18	4
70 Yards 3 shots	51	44	44%	12%	51%	81%	4	4	8	.75	32	3	14	3

a similar hold will kill turkeys *cleanly* to a full seventy yards. And when I say cleanly I mean it is rare for the birds to move on the ground. If you have not examined the wound channel produced by a single copper-plated BB shot, you will be impressed when you first see one. Invariably, there will be a clean channel through the flesh. The effect of BB's on the skeletal structure of game birds is awesome.

Another strategy espoused by some experts is the small-shot followed by heavy-shot idea. This may be an improvement on the number-six-is-best idea, but not by much. The problem with the often-read advice of chambering a number six for the first round, followed by a number four, followed by a number two is that Mr. Gobbler may not decide to put himself at the appropriate range at the appropriate time. Your first chance may often be a shot for which only number two's or BB's will be appropriate! The fact that a number two shot load is in your gun, as a backup, does not help the number six load meet the challenge of a flying turkey at fifty yards. Most experienced hunters realize the best policy is to put the best load in the gun for any chance. I have learned this lesson from several years of problems encountered with a 3-inch number six in the bottom barrel and a 3-inch number two in the top barrel of a Browning over-and-under. In a few cases I selected for the number two's for a fifty-yard chance at a bird that would come no further; however, on flushing birds I was simply not quick enough to use the selector and took quick shots with the number sixes at fifty yards, only to try the number two's when the birds were at sixty or sixty-five yards and out of range.

A final comment concerning large versus small shot is that my advocacy of large shot is made in the context of a shell that can provide adequate pattern density. But *don't forget,* the quantity of large shot must be such that effective pattern density *for a wild turkey* can be delivered.

Careful weighing of all wild turkeys I have harvested indicates an average size of twelve pounds twelve ounces. This average includes my spring gobblers—with an average weight of eighteen pounds three ounces. My birds taken in the fall, most as immature birds of the year, have been much smaller, hence the twelve-pound-plus overall average. A formula I developed from Colonel Burrard's work indicates a twelve-pound, twelve-ounce turkey has approximately sixty-one square inches of vital area. BB pellet counts do not have to be very high to get a significant number of hits to this sixty-one-square inch area. The critical point is that this is not a 2½-pound duck or an eight-pound goose you are trying to hit with BB's! Table Two shows the number of vital hits we can anticipate making use of this vital-area concept. Studies of birds I have killed indicate the number of vital hits made on turkeys will be very close to that estimated by the formula.

In deference to the small-shot advocates, many developed this philosophy when the ability to achieve adequate pattern densities with large shot had not been achieved. Today, modern 12-gauge and 10-gauge loads provide fine performance with three's, two's and BB's. To achieve optimum performance, buffered loads of copper-plated shot are necessary. Number two's and BB's are best *only when appropriate guns and loads* are used. If you argue that your 28-gauge will not pattern them efficiently, I will counter that a turkey gun should be a shotgun that delivers at least 80 percent patterns of at least 1¼-ounce of at least number-three-size shot at forty yards. The gauge, barrel length, and choke will take care of themselves.

THE MODERN 10-GAUGE

The 10-gauge magnum gun has finally come of age in the seventh decade of the twentieth century. Until 1977, there was no decent ammunition available for the 3½-inch chambered guns. The pre-1977 two-ounce load was fifteen years behind the fine magnum 12-gauge loads that were equal or superior to it. Table Four indicates the way in which an improvement in ammunition has altered the performance of the 10-gauge gun. Table Four demonstrates that at 60 yards the best factory load available in 1976 provided half the energy of the best factory load available two years later.

Unfortunately, the reputation of the 10-gauge gun has been damaged by the inferior quality of this pre-1978 factory ammunition. The hand load listed in Table Four demonstrates that spec-

TABLE THREE
10 GAUGE MAGNUM EFFICIENCY vs. 12 GAUGE MAGNUM EFFICIENCY
(same guns as in Tables One and Two)

LOADS

10 gauge Factory Federal Premium Magnum 2¼ oz. Buffered Number BB shot With maximum powder charge	12 gauge Factory Federal Premium Magnum 1⅞ oz. Buffered Number BB shot With maximum powder charge

(Each load is selected because it provides the best long range performance in its respective gun)

	Range - 40 Yards		Range - 60 Yards		Range - 80 Yards		Muzzle velocity (in feet per second) as chronographed
	Number of pellets in 30 inch circle	Foot pounds of energy to vital areas	Number of pellets in 30 inch circle	Foot pounds of energy to vital areas	Number of pellets in 30 inch circle	Foot pounds of energy to vital areas	
Federal Factory 10 gauge 3½ inch mag. 2¼ oz. BB shot	107	135	63	53	29	16	1251
Federal Factory 12 gauge 3 inch mag. 1⅞ oz. BB shot	88	96	55	43	24	11	1137

TABLE FOUR

THE INFLUENCE OF AMMUNITION ON 10 GAUGE PERFORMANCE

(All shells fired in same 10 gauge gun used in Tables One and Two)

	3 SHOTS AT 40 YARDS				3 SHOTS AT 60 YARDS		
	Mean number of pellets in 30 inch circle	Mean percentage of total load in 30 inch circle	Foot pounds of energy to vital areas		Mean number of pellets in 30 inch circle	Mean percentage of total load in 30 inch circle	Foot pounds of energy to vital areas
Best factory load available before 1977: 2 oz. no. 2 shot - no buffer, no copper plated shot, no BB size available	121	65%	82.5		47	25%	24
Best factory load available in 1979: Federal Premium 2¼ oz., buffered, copper plated shot	107	86%	135 *		63	49%	43
Handload: 2⅜ oz. buffered, copper plated shot (This load was used in tables one and two.)	105	90%	135 *		59	51%	53

* These numbers are the same because the greater velocity of the 2⅛ oz. handload produces more individual pellet energy (15 foot pounds per pellet vs. 12).

tacular performance was available to the 10-gauge aficionado before 1978; however, most of the literature concerning the 10-gauge did not address the capabilities of handloads.

The ten-gauge is a superior gauge. As Table Three demonstrates, even the best of the three-inch 12-gauge loads cannot match the currently available factory loads of the 10-gauge.

I am a firm believer in the 10-gauge. My attraction is not based simply on the large quantity of shot it accommodates but also on the superior velocity, and hence greater pellet energy, that 10-gauge loads produce.

Recoil is high. No 10-gauge gun should weigh less than ten pounds. However, if the gun weighs ten to twelve pounds and has a well designed stock, it will not be painful to shoot. In fact, I recently compared the recoil of an eight-pound 12-gauge gun shooting 1⅞-ounce, three-inch magnum loads with a 10½-pound 10-gauge shooting 2¼-ounce, 3½-inch loads. Both loads were the Federal Premiums used in the tests described above. The stock dimensions on both guns were identical. Two experienced shooters fired approximately fifteen rounds with each gun. Both shooters offered the opinion that the eight pound 12-gauge gun developed more painful recoil than the 10 ½-pound 10-gauge gun. The 3½-inch ten gauge gun does kick, and one that weighed under ten pounds would be dangerous for an inexperienced shooter; however, the idea that shooting a 10-gauge double is like being in an automobile accident is nonsense.

THE MOST APPROPRIATE GUN AND LOAD

Now that we have reviewed these data, let us look at the best choice. The most effective load is from 1⅞ to 2½ ounces of copper-plated BB shot propelled at a velocity of between 1250–1300 fps. To attain this velocity with this quantity of shot, one must use a 3½-inch 10-gauge gun. The most effective gun is one that will put 90 percent of such a load in a thirty-inch circle at forty yards and, more importantly, 50 percent in a thirty-inch circle at sixty yards. If you think this cannot be achieved, I ask you to look at the data in Table Two. With this large shot a thirty- or thirty-two-inch barrel with a relatively *modest amount* of full choke constriction is the answer. Many guns are too tightly choked. With a normal bore diameter of .729-inch my best 12-gauge performance has come with between 25 and 30 degrees of constrictions (or 25 or 30 thousandths of an inch less than bore size). In my two 10-gauge Ithaca guns the factory constriction of .041-inch for a choke measurement of .734-inch has provided better pattern than the one opened by three one-thousandths of an inch to .737-inch or .038-inch constriction.

While the above combination is the *most* effective it is certainly not the only good choice. Other choices would include from 1¼ to 1⅞ ounces of number two copper shot at velocities of from 1150 to 1300 fps. That velocity level can be attained with the 1¼ to 1⅜ ounce loads in the 2¾-inch twelve. The 1⅜ to 1⅞ loads can be propelled at adequate velocity in the three-inch 12-gauge gun. Again, optimum pattern performance can be anticipated with thirty-inch barrels of improved modified choke.

In my opinion, a very effective turkey combination can be built in either of these general performance ranges. If the number-two shot loads are used, I believe you have a superb gun to a full fifty-five yards. If the BB, 10-gauge loads are used, that maximum effective range can be extended a full fifteen yards more—to a legitimate seventy yards. In addition, the 10-gauge advantage is not simply one of range. It is excellent at penetrating brush at closer range. In some situations, such as a large gobbler flying directly away in thick cover, the big 10-gauge can help at thirty-five yards.

The turkey hunter or perspective hunter must assess his own capabilities and desires in making a choice between the twelve and the ten. If one shoots a big twelve well I suggest he use it, with the prescribed number-two shot loads, and accept its fifty-five yard capabilities. If you try a 10-gauge and believe you can handle the weight and recoil, you will enjoy a significant advantage; but, if you don't shoot it well the choice is a poor one.

It has been my experience, in two seasons of hunting with Ithaca's big 10-gauge automatic, that you probably will be surprised at how easily the big gun is carried. My first full day in the woods with the gun was a pleasant surprise. The extra three-and-a-half pounds (more than my three-inch twelve) did not prove enervating.

The major problem I have encountered with the gun has been the difficulty in holding it in position while a turkey comes toward my blind. Turkey hunters learn that an attempt to raise a gun after a turkey is in range is usually an error; hence, most of us try to be looking down the barrel as the turkey covers the last twenty yards. The big ten becomes a difficult challenge in these moments. In fact, I now try to build my small blinds so that they support the gun in a semi-mounted position. Needless to say, this procedure is not always effective. The gun is heavy. If your hunting involves difficult climbing and searching for turkeys and if you are not in good physical condition, the additional 3½ pounds will take its toll.

A well choked twelve with copper-plated number two shot also represents a very effective choice. In fact, if you have such a gun you shoot well, I doubt if the gamble that you will be able to shoot the big ten as well is worth the trouble or cost. If you use a twelve, you must make the effort to come up with a good number two copper-plated shot load. All my loads have been developed with Winchester lubaloy shot. There is no question that the lubaloy is significantly superior to the regular BB and number two's. I hand load my shells in both 12 and 10 gauge. For both the 10-gauge and 12-gauge, the Federal Premium load comes close to matching handloads. A very popular load with local turkey hunters is the Winchester XX buffered 12-gauge loads in both 2¾- and 3-inch sizes. While these loads do not have copper shot, they are far superior to all but buffered copper shot loads. I have killed six turkeys with Winchester XX 3-inch magnum loads and believe they are good fifty-yard loads in number two shot. However, I am now a firm believer in copper shot and use it for all my long range loads. The value of copper shot is demonstrated not just in its better pattern but also in improved penetration on game. There is significantly less deformation in turkeys than there is with non-plated shot.

I have not killed a turkey with the new Federal Premium loads but am sure they will prove to be a fine choice. The advantage of the handload is, of course, the ability to tailor it to your particular gun. No commercial shells equal my pet 2⅛-ounce, copper-plated BB 10-gauge load or my 2½-ounce number three shot load. Table Four indicates the superiority of the handload to even the fine Federal Premium load.

I will add one important word of caution with respect to the buffered loads. The buffered *factory* Winchester XX 2¾-inch, 1½-ounce load produced ring bulges at the choke area in a pre-war German drilling. Subsequent tests indicated the bore of the 12-gauge drilling measured only .720-inch; also, the gun had very steep choke constriction. It handled the normal loads but could not accommodate the buffered loads. Some threat may exist with other early guns, or guns of light construction when using the buffered loads. Also, all buffered loads should be handloaded with great care. I weigh every shot and powder charge.

GUN TYPE

Any gun you shoot well that can effectively deliver the loads mentioned above is a good choice. You can argue that the double, be it side-by-side or over-and-under, has the advantage of shorter overall length in the blind. All other things being equal, the compactness is an advantage. In addition, I enjoy the fact that I can slip two shells in a double with virtually no noise. I really have trouble trying to get shells into the big Ithaca 10-gauge without some metallic clicks. On a still spring morning, Mr. Turkey does not tolerate many metallic clicks. So, the quietness of the double is an advantage. Also, I never have had a mechanical failure with my doubles as I have with the automatics.

The single most important advantage of the double, or over and under, is that it gives you a choice of choke and shot size. This choice can be a particular advantage in wild turkey hunting. I now hunt with a 2½-ounce number three load in my right barrel and the 2⅛-ounce BB load in the left barrel of my 10-gauge Beretta double. The degree of choke constriction is the same but the nature of the handloaded shells results in the BB load producing 90-percent-plus patterns at forty yards while the number three load achieves 66 percent patterns. If the bird is close, the number three load is a distinct advantage. If the bird is fifty-five yards or more away, or if he is in dense brush, or if he is flying directly away at modest range, the BB load is superior. In most situations, it is the ability to select the wide pattern of the number three load at close range that makes this choice a particularly valuable one. The BB load, or any of the tight buffered loads, make hitting a moving or flying target at close range significantly more difficult. This is true of buffered loads with all shot sizes. A buffered load of copper-plated number six shot provides a dense, tight pattern. At close range it is tougher to hit with this load than it is with a nice 66 percent pattern of number three's. Small shot itself does not guarantee that you will have wide pellet dispersion.

I firmly believe that the tremendous advantage of two *shotgun* shots over one makes the combination shotgun/over-under/rifle a poor choice. I hunted with such a combination gun, and killed turkeys with it; however, I sold it after I watched too many turkeys pop up in good range after I had missed one difficult shot with the shotgun.

Ah, I have not mentioned the drilling. Many suggest it is the perfect turkey gun. I have a beautiful pre-war drilling in 12 gauge over 8x57 JR. caliber with a 1.5 x 5x Leupold scope mounted by Paul Jaeger of Jenkintown, Pennsylvania. It shoots 2-inch groups at one hundred yards with the 8x57 mm and only weighs 8¼ pounds with the scope. It is a very effective gun; however, a drilling is only effective if you can shoot the shotgun barrels well. That is, such guns must be well stocked; it will probably take some work to adjust their knife-blade combs. I still get a sick feeling in my stomach when reflecting upon the punishment I took from a 3-inch mag 12 over-under gun that weighed 6½ pounds and had a comb about 1/16 of an inch in width! If you get a drilling you shoot well it can make a very nice turkey gun, although the complexity of the Greener type safety and barrel selector will probably cause you more trouble than you would suspect. One distinct advantage of my drilling is, believe it or not, the scope. Birds that come into a call will often present a small target; also the cross hairs, and the *light-gathering* power of the scope; are great advantages. Before slapping a scope on a big shotgun you have to be conscious of the danger of recoil of any other than a long-eye relief scope. In addition, the fact that for wing shots the scope may be a serious disadvantage should be considered.

In summary, my general advice is: find a gun that puts 80 percent or more of at least 1¼ ounces of at least number two shot in a 30-inch circle at forty yards. Make sure you can shoot the gun well and that it provides at least two quick shots. If you can handle more weight, recoil, and cost, select a big 10 gauge and use heavy loads of at least size three shot.

In all cases, realize the vitality and grandeur of this bird and avoid taking a shot at a bird out of range. A turkey at a hundred yards looks close—no shotgun should be fired at a turkey at eighty yards, let alone one hundred. A clean kill of a turkey is immensely satisfying; however, I would suggest that a measure of satisfaction can be taken from having the character to refuse the eighty-yard shot when you have a gun that you know might kill one at that range. The wild turkey deserves no less from the hunter.

PART TWO: THE RIFLE

The American hunter's love affair for accurate and esthetically pleasing rifles is well documented.

The turkey is the only American game bird for which a small group of riflemen have developed equipment and techniques. In most areas, the shotgun is significantly more popular and, in the hands of most hunters, more efficient. The primary exception is found in the arid and open West, where many sporting opportunities are available for the rifle.

In any area, the contemptible meat hunter can find opportunities to assassinate birds on the roost or feeding in open fields at varmint shooting ranges. The discussion that follows relates to the sporting use of rifles. It is the purpose of this section to both identify what constitutes the most efficient wild turkey cartridge and to comment on the way a variety of cartridges can be adapted to the bird.

THE HORRORS OF TOO MUCH GUN OR TOO LITTLE GUN

As mentioned in the section on shotguns, the wild turkey is very hard to kill. The 22-rimfire cartridge, including the high-speed, light-projectile 22 cartridges, is simply not an adequate turkey cartridge. I suspect even highly experienced turkey hunters would be horrified at the number of birds that have been lost after being hit with the various rimfire cartridges.

The 22-rimfire magnum has achieved some popularity among turkey hunters. The 40-grain bullet at 2000 feet per second (fps) velocity produces much greater energy than the various 22-long rifle cartridges. However, this cartridge is also a marginal performer. It is frequently marginal not only in terms of energy at the 100- and 150-yard ranges but also in terms of the accuracy the cartridge achieves in many of the guns chambered for it. Our discussion will not include any of these rimfire cartridges.

I have also witnessed cases where too much energy has been used in killing a turkey. Too many turkeys are being mutilated by hunters with high-velocity rifles shooting bullets designed for varmints or deer. This is not simply a problem of meat destruction; turkeys should be killed efficiently and neatly—period. Even when meat destruction is not great, only the most callous of hunters could enjoy carrying a disemboweled turkey from the woods.

The cartridges which are the worst culprits in the context of destruction are the popular high speed 6mms, the 25-06, and the great 270 Winchester with its 130-grain bullet. I have seen far too many birds mutilated by these cartridges. Hunters that hold for the body of turkeys using these cartridges with full power loads are committing a crime.

CENTER-FIRE CARTRIDGE PERFORMANCE

The most comprehensive and lucid discussion of cartridges and turkey hunting was published by Davis in his 1949 work, *The American Wild Turkey*. He provides data on the results of numerous kills with a variety of calibers and rifles. It is the aim of this section to provide detailed comments on my field experiences and experiments with a variety of cartridges which are widely used in hunting turkeys. Data collected from kills made by me and hunters I have guided are supplemented by autopsies conducted on a variety of small game I have killed with loads developed for turkey hunting.

THE SMALL CASE TWENTY-TWO CALIBER CENTER-FIRE CARTRIDGE

Traditionally, the 22 Hornet has been called the perfect wild turkey cartridge—a comment often made as a digression by those writing about varmint rifles. The small Hornet is a very efficient cartridge. Other 22-caliber cartridges of relatively small case size include the 218 Bee, the 222 Remington, the 223 Remington, and the 222 Remington Magnum. All these cartridges can accommodate efficient loads. In general, the efficient load for this class of cartridges is one which propels a 45- to 55-grain bullet at between 2200 and 2700 fps muzzle velocity.

TESTS: THE 22 HORNET AND THE 222 REMINGTON

These two cartridges can be developed into supremely efficient turkey loads. The Hornet is unquestionably the superior cartridge in factory loaded ammunition. Depending on the manufacture, the Hornet 45 grain expanding bullet provides between 2400 and 2700 fps from most rifles. This load is an efficient killer that is not too destructive. In most cases, the accuracy of the factory load can be improved upon with a handload tailored to one's particular rifle. In a good rifle, the Hornet factory load will usually shoot between 1½- and 2-inch groups at one hundred yards. My best handload, a 50-grain Remington .224 match bullet and 11.5 grains of Winchester 680 powder, shrinks that to an honest 1 inch. The average velocity of that load, as documented on my chronograph, is 2602 fps from a 24-inch barrel of a Model 70 Winchester.

The 222 Remington is also a great turkey cartridge. In factory loads, the expanding bullet is much too explosive when used at normal turkey hunting ranges. The metal-cased factory bullet is too destructive and, in my guns, has not achieved the accuracy for which the 222 is justifiably praised. The 222 can be loaded down to the sub 2700 fps range without sacrificing its great accuracy.

My best load has been a 52-grain Sierra hollow point boat-tail match bullet with 20.0 grains of Winchester 748 powder. Average velocity is 2603 fps in a 23″ barrel of a SAKO rifle. It is highly accurate, averaging about ¾″ groups at 100 yards.

PERFORMANCE ON GAME

As would be expected from the similarities in velocity and bullet weight, the 22 Hornet and 222 handloads are comparable in killing power. The 222 is slightly more destructive than the 22 Hornet, although, it is not overly so.

Tests on groundhogs show that at typical turkey hunting ranges, of 40–150 yards, the two will produce around .50- to .90-inch caliber exit holes. Heavy tissue destruction will extend for a direction of about 2 inches around the path of the bullet. The 222 wounds will be almost exactly identical to the Hornet at about 50 yards greater range. The handloaded 222 at 150 yards is tough to distinguish from a Hornet wound at 100 yards. If heavy bone is hit, the destruction will be more severe but is still not too great.

Any solid hit in the forward part of the body will anchor a groundhog on the spot. The kill is usually very quick and clean. In contrast, the 222 factory metal-case cartridge tears up turkeys and groundhogs. Chronographed at above 2900 fps, it is just too fast.

GENERAL COMMENTS ON THIS CLASS OF CARTRIDGE

If you do not handload, the 22 Hornet is still your best choice as a turkey cartridge. Any cartridge in this range can be an efficient turkey round. When working up loads, stay within the 2400–2600 fps velocity range. From tests with other calibers, I am sure that the small, .224-inch diameters of the bullets is a factor contributing to the lack of destruction of this class of cartridge. It is not just a function of velocity and bullet construction. As will be noted below, larger caliber and heavier bullets will tend to be more destructive regardless of their velocities or bullet constructions.

These cartridges are quiet and fun to shoot. Also, despite the fact that one-inch accuracy is poor in terms of the state of the art of bench-rest shooting, a rifle that consistently places its bullets within an inch at 100 yards provides accuracy that seems phenomenal when shooting in the field is done at under 150 yards. When I do my part, with my old pre-1964 model 70 Winchester Hornet, the bullet seems to land exactly where the crosshairs of the scope are placed. One word of caution to the individual who will use the 22 Hornet. It has been my experience that the development of accurate loads will be much more time consuming in the 22 Hornet than in the 222 Remington or most other cartridges. Some experimentation with .223-inch as well as .224-inch diameter bullets is frequently demanded. Also, many good .224-inch bullets of over 50 grains in weight will not shoot well in the Hornet's 1-in-16-inch twist barrel.

THE LARGE CASE 22-CALIBER VARMINT RIFLES

The 22-250, 225 Winchester, and the 220 Swift all can be handloaded to produce velocities in the 2,000 foot range; however, the large case does make light load development more difficult.

TEST: 220 SWIFT

The great 220 Swift, perhaps the most unfairly maligned cartridge of our time, can be loaded down efficiently. My Swift load is 13.0 grains of 4759 powder and the 55 Sierra Spitzer bullet. This groups in about 1½ inch at one hundred yards from a very accurate model 70 Winchester (the same rifle consistently averages ½-inch groups with full loads and match bullets). The velocity of the light load is right at 2100 fps.

PERFORMANCE ON GAME

I find this load to be less efficient than those of the 22 Hornet and the 222 Remington. The most obvious problem is in the accuracy—the 1½-inch load was developed after considerable, and frustrating, experimentation. Wound channels are quite similar to those produced by the Hornet and the 222. The only difference is that every once in a while a wound will be more damaging.

Given the nature of the rifles for which they are chambered, it is unlikely these cartridges would ever be developed for turkeys. Most such guns are heavy and longer; my model 70, for example, has a 26-inch barrel.

THE COMBINATION VARMINT/MEDIUM GAME CARTRIDGES

The class of cartridges which can be used for both varmints and medium-sized game such as deer and antelope enjoy tremendous popularity. They are generally accurate, pleasant to shoot and efficient killers of game for which they are designed. Included in this category would be the 243 Winchester, 244 Remington, 6mm-Remington, 250-3000, 257 Roberts, and the 25-06.

Fine turkey load can be developed for cartridges within this class. Factory loads are not applicable to turkey hunting. In fact, this is the class of cartridges responsible for more shattered turkeys than any other. The popularity of cartridges within this category is impressive. Also, due to the inherent accuracy of the cartridges and the fact that most rifles in this range are equipped with scope sights, and average hunter has a good chance of hitting a turkey. In no case should a factory load be selected for use.

Handloads developed in the 2000–2500 fps velocity range and utilizing metal-jacket bullets can produce efficient loads. Generally the step up to the .243-inch caliber and the doubling of bullet weight from the .224-inch cartridges makes the metal-cased bullet the best choice.

TESTS: THE 243 WINCHESTER AND 25-06 REMINGTON

These two cartridges are at extreme ends of the combination gun spectrum. The little 243 case is well suited to reduced loads. The big 25-06 case is not; however, both cartridges can be loaded to the 2000–2500 fps range. Metal jacket bullets are readily available for the .243-inch caliber but not for the .257-inch diameter bullet of the 25-06. A fine load for the 243 is 26.0 of 4064 powder and the 90-grain Speer metal-jacketed bullet. It averages 2300 fps in a 24-inch-barrel gun and provides 1¼-inch accuracy at one hundred yards. Also, it strikes the target within about 2-inches of full power load. Unfortunately, and as is frequently the case with reduced loads, its impact is not only lower than the normal load but about 1½ inches to the left; hence a slight sight adjustment is necessary for accurate shooting.

The 25-06 reduced load is 19.0 grains of 4759 powder and the Sierra 100 grain, .257-inch, Spitzer bullet. It produces 1-inch accuracy in a very accurate Savage 112 V. varmint rifle. This load strikes the target three inches below a full power, 100-grain load that averages 3350 fps velocity. Unlike the .243 Winchester, the light load is directly below the full power load.

PERFORMANCE ON GAME

The light load in the .243 with a metal-jacketed bullet is a good turkey load. On groundhogs, the exit hole will be only 40 to 60 caliber at ranges of 50 to 175 yards. The entrance hole is noticeably larger than the .224-inch bullet. The wound channel will be about 2-inches in diameter. Unfortunately the bullet may tumble if it strikes heavy bone and, occasionally, a destructive wound will be produced. Interestingly, these loads do not seem to anchor either groundhogs or turkeys quite as well as the faster .224-inch loads with expanding bullets.

The .264 to .323 Caliber Moderate Velocity Medium Game Cartridges

Included in this category would be the 270 Winchester, 280 Remington, 7mm, 264 Winchester, 30-06, and 8 x 57 mm.

All of these cartridges are too large to be optimum for turkeys; however, relatively efficient light loads can be developed for them.

TESTS: THE 270 WINCHESTER AND THE 8 X 57 MM

The gun pictured was designed to be an all-around rifle for North American hunting. Despite the fact it is of 270 caliber, I have killed more turkeys with it than any other rifle. It is highly accurate, compact, and efficient. My turkey load is 22.0 grains of 4759 powder with the 110 Sierra bullet. Velocity will average about 2000 fps. In the 8 x 57 mm, I have used a load that produces sub 2000 fps velocity yet works well. The load is 26 grains of

4759 powder and the 196-grain R.W.S. H-mantle bullet. Average velocity is 1700 fps and it averages 1½-minute-of-angle accuracy from a pre-war German drilling.

PERFORMANCE ON GAME

The 110 Sierra is, surprisingly, not too destructive. If heavy bone is hit, a good bit of tissue will be destroyed, but with properly placed bullets the wounds are not bad. Typical wounds will show 75 to 85-caliber exit holes and 2½-inch tissue damage channel along the path of the bullet. My experiments with the 270 taught me that heavy expanding bullets, designed for heavy game, are not necessarily the answer. I loaded the big 170-grain Speers with 4759 powder to produce about 2000 fps velocity. These *did not* punch a neat clean hole, despite what you might expect. The destruction caused by these bullets was much greater than the 110 Sierras. Even on a number of squirrels I shot with these, the wounds were large. I suspect the problem is the tendency of the bullet to tumble after it hits the target. In any event, the most destruction I have examined at the 2000 fps velocity level was caused by the 170 Speers from the 270. Again, this is not destruction like that of any of the 3000 fps cartridges, but it is still too much.

If you are a one-gun man, the use of 4759 powder allows some nice circa-2000 foot loads which will shoot well and, with good bullet placement, not tear a turkey apart.

THE "DEER RIFLE" CARTRIDGES—MEDIUM BORES AT RELATIVELY LOW VELOCITY

The 30-30, 32 Winchester and 35 Remington. If your gun has adequate accuracy, these cartridges are really good choices for turkeys. Killing power is fine and, with good bullet placement, destruction of tissue is not too severe. One of the neatest wild turkey kills I ever witnessed was made by a friend with a factory 30-30 load in a German drilling. The factory loads with a lot of lead exposed at the tip of the bullet are not as good as those with some controlled expansion such as the Winchester Silver Tip or Remington Core Lokt. With this class of cartridge your bullet placement must be good or significant destruction of tissue will result.

PERFORMANCE ON GAME

This class of cartridge will normally make a large, 3-inch, wound channel through the bird. The exit hole will be about 150 caliber. There is none of the explosive, hydraulic effect of the 3000+ fps cartridge, but neither is there the neat narrow wound of the 2500 ± fps .224 caliber. The energy of this cartridge is good, and it is rare that a well hit bird will be lost.

Experiments with various types of bullets may be valuable in these cartridges, as some are not nearly as destructive as others. Also, loading bullets of 30 caliber designed for faster cartridges is a good idea. The velocity of factory cartridges, about 2100–2200 fps, is about right. You can go a bit lower, but then the trajectory becomes a problem when trying to hit a bird at 125 yards.

THE LARGE CASE MAGNUM CARTRIDGES OF 30 CALIBER AND UNDER

Despite the fact that these cartridges would be a poor choice specifically for turkey hunting, we will discuss them here because some American hunters have selected one as their single all-around cartridge. Included in this category would be the 7mm Remington Magnum, the 300 H&H Magnum and the 300 Winchester Magnum.

Turkey loads can be developed for these cartridges by using metal-jacketed bullets at 2000–2200 fps.

TEST: THE 300 WINCHESTER MAGNUM

This massive cartridge can be loaded to modest velocities. The best load I have developed is 20 grains of 4759 powder and a 185-grain Speer match bullet.

The accuracy of this load is good, averaging about 2-inches in a model 70 Winchester. Also, with good bullet placement, tissue destruction is not too great. One problem with this class of cartridge is that the light load will often strike the target far from the full-power load. My light load strikes the target nine inches below my full-power 3000+ fps 180-grain load.

CONCLUSIONS CONCERNING THE RIFLE FOR WILD TURKEYS

The best rifle to use for the hunting of wild turkeys is a .224 caliber, center-fire cartridge with an expanding bullet at between 2400 and 2600 fps. It is most probable that requisite accuracy for such a load, which we will call 1½ minute of angle, will be achieved in one of the small-case 22 caliber cartridges designed for varmint hunting at less than 250 yards. The type of rifle that will regularly produce such accuracy will be either a bolt action or a single shot. The weight of the rifle, barrel length, and stock design are a matter of personal preference.

For the one-rifle man, a cartridge in the 6mm range can be well adapted to turkey hunting.

The information provided above also indicates that a wide range of cartridges which were not designed for turkeys can be tailored to this species of game.

· 8 ·

The Future

It is ironic that the bird which under fair-chase conditions is the most challenging of North American game can be killed easily by unscrupulous hunters. The wariest of turkeys can be assassinated on its roost, shot at long range in open fields, and butchered over bait. With the exception of baiting, these acts often qualify as legal hunting techniques under the rules imposed by some states. Even if there are no laws against roost-shooting or sniping at long range with varmint rifles, the acts should be condemned.

The fair-chase philosophy is not necessarily adopted by those who follow game laws to the letter; moreover, there are those who have violated game laws and yet follow the fair-chase philosophy. It is a crime to shoot any turkey off the roost, whether a states' game laws allow it or not.

A turkey hunter with a measure of integrity will take his birds in an honorable manner. Opportunities that provide no challenge should be passed up. The attractions of the hunt is in meeting the challenge of predicting the bird's behavior or in fooling him. Satisfaction should be derived from the success with which this is achieved. Killing the bird should only be rewarding when it is the culminating step in meeting significant challenges. Killing alone is meaningless and obscene. Unfortunately, public acknowledgement of the hunter's accomplishments, and the prestige he derives from them, is generally allocated exclusively on the basis of killing turkeys—not on an appraisal of the challenges met. The turkey taken in fair chase looks no different than the one shot over bait.

Turkey hunters must accept the fact that there are men that

shoot birds from cars, off the roost, and over bait. Their well-timed visits to checking stations and lies about their exploits in public places establish a reputation for them. Most will never be publicly embarrassed for their deeds. There is no easy way to expose them as exaggerators, liars, and cheaters.

Let the phony enjoy the empty praise of the ignorant. He will live with the cheap kills, lies and deceptions, until they color his character.

From a positive perspective, take pride in adhering to a fair-chase philosophy. Allow it to become a dominant aspect in your enjoyment. This philosophy does not stop at refusing to undertake the unethical, but rather can be developed so that ethical and yet essentially meaningless kills are passed up. There is nothing unethical about shooting a bird that flushes at your feet as you search for the flock in the fall, but what satisfaction is derived from killing the bird? This is no accomplishment for an experienced hunter. It is not that the shot is too easy, for the bird you call to your blind may present an easier chance; however, the point is the latter opportunity has been created by your effort and skill and the former is a result of chance. Strive to make your kills an accomplishment you can learn from.

Don't misunderstand the difficulties implicit in adhering to the fair chase philosophy. After a week of hard hunting in the fall, when all your friends are bringing turkeys home, the temptation to put any turkey on the table is great. Those of us who have succumbed to that temptation have failed to recognize that the accomplishment is not in killing but in killing under the conditions we set.

A great warmth and sense of accomplishment derives from doing it the right way, particularly after passing up opportunities that present no significant challenge.

PART TWO: WHAT YOU CAN DO ON BEHALF
OF THE WILD TURKEY

Every hunter has the capacity to benefit the wild turkey. In fact, each of us should have the goal of making a contribution to helping assure the future success of turkey populations. Personal greed, economic necessity, stupidity, and a lack of appreciation of the value of maintaining turkey habitat are major threats to the wild turkey's future. Habitat deterioration is a particular threat to the wild turkey. Unlike many other forms of game, our bird will not tolerate significant alterations in its habitat. Deer adjust to tremendous increases in human population; turkeys will not. We must strive to maintain large areas of woods and swamps.

Maintaining wild areas will not be easy and it will not be inexpensive, but it can be accomplished. The success of Ducks Unlimited provides a concrete example of the progress that can be realized when hunters band together to a common goal.

Each of us, even when unaffiliated with a major organization, can make a valuable contribution. Most of us hunt on private land. Many landowners will be receptive to the idea of planting shrubs that are beneficial to wildlife. I have yet to encounter a landowner who denied me permission to plant autumn olive at a few strategic spots in their woods. The state wildlife agencies and many private organizations oriented to conservation will provide advice and assistance in acquiring plants and trees.

If a hunter is fortunate enough to own a tract of land himself, or have a significant track in his family, there is almost no limit to what he can accomplish. On two hundred acres which I own in West Virginia I have received help from the state in planting literally thousands of autumn olives, building a pond, and establishing a block of white pines. The area in which these changes were implemented now enjoys significantly greater use by a variety of wildlife, including turkeys.

If you are a member of a hunt club you should urge that time, effort, and money be committed to the development of your property for wildlife. Often, timber management can result in improving the attractiveness of an area to game. Many hunt camps have existed for decades without making a major effort to improve their property for game. Frequently, this results from an ordering of priorities that places planting shrubs for wildlife well below mowing the grass around cabins during the summer. The club is particularly well suited to the development of effective programs because a labor force of individuals with at least some measure of interest in the game on the property is readily available. Education may be an important step to achieving greater contributions to habitat improvement from those of us who belong to camps. Many members still believe that harvesting any timber reduces the area's attractiveness to all game; consequently, many camps do not have enough open land. Turkeys and virtually all other forms of game derive benefit from small clearings. Wildlife management personnel preach the value of open areas in all their literature. The need is to get the message to the men who can put it to use.

In the context of hunt clubs and other organizations, each of us has the obligation to strive to see that the fair-chase ethic is supported. Imposing even more demanding rules than those articulated by the law is another positive step. A gobblers-only philosophy can be adopted by a club in the fall season in states which allow hens to be harvested. In some areas such a policy may not be necessary, but it is hard to imagine that it would be detrimental to a population.

The establishment and growth of the Wild Turkey Federation is an encouraging sign for the wild turkey. Hopefully, this organization will prove to be as beneficial for the turkey as Ducks Unlimited has been for waterfowl. The publication of a journal, *Turkey Call,* has provided for more regular communication among hunters and has helped disseminate valuable information. Support of research and programs oriented to habitat maintenance and improvement have been exercised. All turkey hunters should join this organization and attempt to play a role in seeing that the highest priority is given to programs relevant to the future welfare of wild turkey populations.

The turkey hunter should seek out and support individuals and groups working to maintain habitat for other species. Ducks Unlimited, Trout Unlimited, and many other groups are working to preserve habitat that pays dividends to wild turkeys. In the area in which I hunt, trout fishermen have been much more effective than turkey hunters in campaigning for the preservation of habitat that will be used by wild turkey populations. To date in my area, turkey hunters have not been effective spokesmen for habitat protection. Hopefully, the Wild Turkey Federation will provide leadership in this area. Calling contests and movies are entertaining and informative, but we need more meetings oriented to encouraging hunters to get involved in political activity relevant to the protection of wild turkey habitat.

Contributions of time and money should be matched by the investment of concern for the reputation of the turkey. The hunter should not tolerate degrading and inaccurate statements about the bird. I make it clear to people that the "he sure is ugly" comment, directed to a recently killed gobbler, is a quick way of making the hunt their last with me.

The status of wild turkeys will be enhanced by increased license fees. The turkey should be considered big game. Each bird should also be accorded the respect of being checked at a game checking station, as is customarily done with deer. In the context of rules and regulations concerning hunting, it is unfortunate that many states allow turkeys to be killed at the same time as small game. Turkeys should be harvested by hunters who are hunting turkeys. The rabbit or squirrel hunter who blunders into a flock of turkeys is not turkey hunting. The concept that wild sheep are not legal game for a rabbit hunter who happens to encounter one seems axiomatic, but we allow rabbit hunters to kill turkeys. I sincerely believe a mature gobbler with 1½-inch spurs and a 10-inch beard is as fine a North American trophy as a Stone Sheep with 40-inch horns. Both the sheep and the turkey should only be harvested by men who are purposefully hunting them.

I deplore the early squirrel seasons that exist in many areas inhabited by wild turkeys. The early seasons encourage the poaching of wild turkeys. I will be quick to add that there are many responsible squirrel hunters who would not consider killing the turkeys they frequently encounter; however, no one can dispute that the seasons allow hunters to be in turkey range before the turkey season opens. Turkeys are killed during this period. I can't estimate how many are killed in the areas I hunt, but I hope there are fewer than I suspect.

All hunters should encourage the enactment and enforcement

of tough laws concerning free roaming dogs and cats. Feral dogs constitute a terrible threat to wild turkey broods in the early summer. In some areas, dogs that destroy turkeys live on farms. Both types of dogs constitute a significant threat; moreover, it is certain that this threat will increase in the future.

The turkey hunter has an obligation to become involved in debating provocative questions with implications for the bird's future. Taking a stand on many of these questions will not be easy, and at times good friends may be alienated. The reward for your effort will come when on some hot summer day you watch a proud hen as she oversees her large brood in a clearing you helped cut and seed. You may be able to take satisfaction in the fact that the hen could be a bird you passed up the fall before. The large brood suggests that the control of wild dogs that you helped encourage and implement may be paying dividends. The enjoyment you will derive from the health of the hen and her brood is a direct contradiction of the often heard criticism that hunters are only interested in the welfare of game to the end that there will be more birds to shoot. Show me the man or woman who is most interested in the welfare of wild turkeys, and who is most willing to make significant investments to that end, and I will introduce you to a wild turkey hunter.

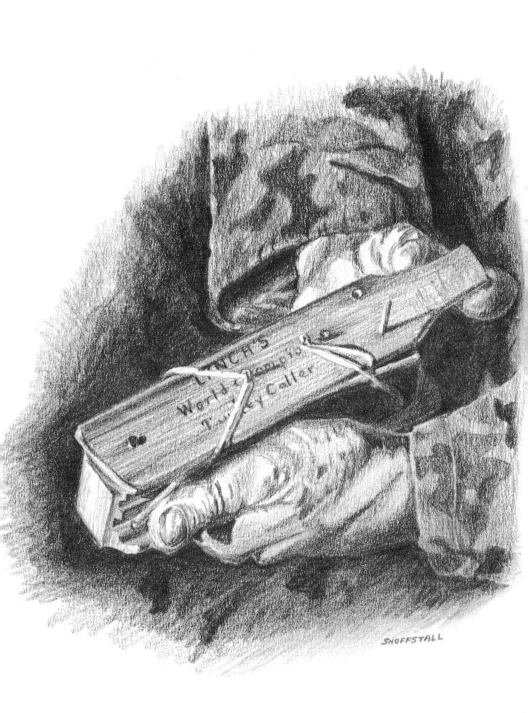

Selected Bibliography

Brady, James F.
    1973   *Modern Turkey Hunting.* New York: Crown Publisher.

Burrard, Major Gerald
    1931   *The Modern Shotgun.* New York: Scribners (3 volumes)

Coggin, J. and C. Peery.
    1975   *The Wild Turkey in Virginia.* Richmond, Virginia: Virginia Commission of Game and Inland Fisheries.

Davis, Henry E.
    1949   *The American Wild Turkey.* Georgetown, South Carolina: Small Arms Technical Publishing Company.

———.

    1950   "Hunting Wild Turkeys with a Rifle" in Charles S. Landis (ed.), *Hunting with the Twenty-Two.* Georgetown, South Carolina: Small Arms Technical Publishing Company.

Elliott, Charles.
    1979   *Turkey Hunting with Charlie Elliott.* New York: David McKay Company.

Everitt, Simon W.
    1928   *Tales of Wild Turkey Hunting.* Chicago: William C. Hazelton Publisher.

Gooch, Bob
    1978   *In Search of Wild Turkey.* Waukegan, Illinois: Greatlakes Living Press, Ltd.

Hanenkrat, William Frank
    1974   *The Education of a Turkey Hunter.* New York: The Winchester Press.

Harbour, Dave
    1975   *Hunting the American Wild Turkey.* Harrisburg, Pa.: Stackpole Books.

Johenning, Leon
    no date   *The Turkey Hunters Guide.* Waynesboro, Va.: The Humphries Press.

Kelly, Tom
    1973   *Tenth Legion.* Monroe, Louisiana: Spur Enterprises.

Latham, Roger M.
    1956   *Complete Book of the Wild Turkey.* Harrisburg, Pa.: Stackpole Books.

McIlhenny, E. A.
    1914   *The Wild Turkey and Its Hunting.* New York: Doubleday & Co.

Mosby, H., and C. Handley
    1943   *The Wild Turkey in Virginia.* Richmond, Va.: Commission of Game and Inland Fisheries.

Schorger, A. W.
    1966   *The Wild Turkey.* Norman, Oklahoma: University of Oklahoma Press.

Turpin, Tom
    1966   *Hunting the Wild Turkey.* Delmont, Pa.: Penns Woods (Reprint of original)

Wheeler, Robert J.
    1948   *The Wild Turkey in Alabama.* Montgomery, Ala.: Alabama Department of Conservation.

Whittington
    1971   *Tall Timber Gabriels.*

NOTES

NOTES